SLEUTH

SLEUTH

Sleuth has all the ingredients of a top-class thriller, which it undoubtedly is—a plot whose twists and surprises are breathtakingly audacious and fiendishly cunning: suspense and excitement galore: and a staggering denouement. Yet it is far more than just that: it is also a brilliant parody of the Agatha Christie country-house thriller, mercilessly satirising the genre at the same time as using its technical devices to the full: it is a dramatic study of sexual conflict and jealousy between an older and a younger man: and finally, it is a subtle psychological study of an inadequate and sexually-obsessed middle-aged man. Clifford Williams' production of the play, which opened at the St. Martin's Theatre, London, in February, 1970, with Anthony Quayle and Keith Baxter in the leading roles, received rave notices from the critics. The play has since been successfully produced in Australia, Sweden and the U.S.

Anthony Shaffer graduated from Cambridge in 1950, where he edited the university magazine *Granta*. After a spell as a barrister, he decided to enter journalism and started writing commercials and documentaries. He also wrote several television plays which were screened, including *Pig in the Middle* and *The Savage Parade*. He has written three screenplays, including *Fourbush and the Penguins* (now being filmed with John Hurt), an adaptation of his brother, Peter Shaffer's stage hit *Black Comedy* and *Play With A Gypsy*, an intellectual horror film.

PLAYSCRIPT 46

'sleuth'

anthony shaffer

MARION BOYARS · LONDON

A MARION BOYARS BOOK
distributed by Calder & Boyars Ltd
18 Brewer Street, London W1R 4AS

First published in Great Britain in 1971
by Calder & Boyars Ltd

Reprinted, illustrated edition, 1973

Reprinted, illustrated edition, 1977
by Marion Boyars Publishers Ltd
18 Brewer Street, London W1R 4AS

All performing rights in this play are strictly reserved
and application for performances should be made to:
Fraser & Dunlop Scripts Ltd
91 Regent Street, London W1

No performance of the play may be given unless a licence
has been obtained prior to rehearsal.

Printed in the United States of America

To: Father Brown, Mr. Philip Trent, Mr. Max Carrados, Dr. Reginald Fortune, Mr. Roger Sheringham, Mr. Albert Campion, Mr. Nigel Strangeways, Lord Peter Wimsey, Dr. Gideon Fell, Monsieur Hercule Poirot, and all their omniscient, eccentric, amateur gentlemen colleagues, this play is dedicated with sincere regard and affection.

Illustrations from the

Palomar Pictures Production of

SLEUTH

Presented by 20th Century-Fox

starring

Laurence Olivier and Michael Caine

screenplay

Anthony Shaffer based upon his play

Produced by Morton Gottlieb

Directed by Joseph L. Mankiewicz

Released in the United Kingdom by
Fox-Rank Distributors Ltd.

SLEUTH

SLEUTH was first presented at the St. Martin's Theatre,
London, on February 12th, 1970, after a pre-London tour of
Oxford, Leeds, Brighton and Eastbourne, with the following cast:

ANDREW WYKE   Anthony Quayle

MILO TINDLE   Keith Baxter

INSPECTOR DOPPLER   Stanley Rushton

DET. SGT. TARRANT   Robin Mayfield

P. C. HIGGS   Liam McNulty

The play was directed by Clifford Williams.

ACT ONE

(The curtain rises on the living room of ANDREW WYKE's Norman Manor House in Wiltshire. It is stone flagged, and a tall window runs the height of the back wall. It is divided laterally by a minstrels gallery which, in turn, is approached by a winding staircase. A wardrobe, stage left, and a grandfather clock, and bureau stage right stand on the gallery. Upstage right is the hallway leading to the unseen front door. Upstage left a corridor leads into another part of the house. Standing in this corridor is a basket. Games of all kinds adorn the room ranging in complexity from chess, draughts and chequers, to early dice and card games and even earlier blocking games like Senat and Nine Men Morris. Upstage centre, by the window, under the gallery is a full-sized "Laughing Sailor."

As the play opens ANDREW WYKE, is sitting at his desk, typing. He is a strongly built, tall, fleshy man of 57, gone slightly to seed. His fair hair carries on it the suspicion that chemical aid has been invoked to keep the grey at bay. His face, sourly amused and shadowed with evaded self-knowledge is beginning to reflect the absence of constant, ardous employment. He wears a smoking jacket and black tie.

The clock strikes eight o'clock. ANDREW turns to look at clock, finishes typing, takes the page from the typewriter and begins to read)

ANDREW. "Since you appear to know so much, Lord
Merridew, Sir," said the Inspector humbly, "I wonder if
you could explain just how the murderer managed to
leave the body of his victim in the middle of the Tennis
Court, and effect his escape without leaving any tracks
behind him in the red dust. Frankly, sir, we in the Police
Force are just plain baffled. There seems no way he could
have done it, short of black magic." St. John Lord
Merridew, the great detective, rose majestically, his huge
Father Christmas face, glowing with mischievous delight.
Slowly he brushed the crumbs of seedy cake from the
folds of his pendulous waistcoat. "The police may be
baffled, Inspector," he boomed, "but Merridew is not. It's
all a question of a little research and a little ratiocination.
Thirty years ago, the murderer, Doctor Grayson, was a
distinguished member of the Ballet Russe dancing under
the name of Oleg Graysinski. The years may have altered
his appearance, but his old skill had not deserted him. He
carried the body out to the centre of the tennis court,
walking on his points along the white tape which divides
the services boxes. From there he threw it five feet into
the court, towards the base line, where it was found, and
then, with a neatly executed fouette, faced about and
returned the way he had come, thus leaving no traces.
There, Inspector, that is Merridew's solution."

Splendid! Absolutely splendid! Merridew loses none of his
cunning I'm glad to say. He's as neat *and* as gaudy as ever
he was.

(The doorbell rings. ANDREW finishes his drink slowly,
then exits to hallway)

Oh hallo. Good evening, Milo Tindle, is it?

MILO. Yes. Mr. Wyke?

ANDREW. Yes. Do come in won't you?

3

MILO.   Thank you.

(The front door is heard to close. ANDREW walks back
into the room. He is followed by MILO TINDLE. He is
about 35, slim, dark-haired and of medium height. He has
a sharp, sallow face alive with a faintly Mediterranean
wariness. Everything about him is neat from his exactly
parted hair to the squared off white handkerchief in the
breast pocket of his blue mohair suit)

ANDREW.   Let me take your coat.

(ANDREW hangs coat on coat rack upstage left)

Did you find the entrance to the lane alright?

MILO.   Yes.

(MILO walks about surveying room)

ANDREW.   Well done. Most people go straight past it. It's
very nice of you to come.

MILO.   Not at all. I found your note when I got down from
London this afternoon.

ANDREW.   Oh good. I pushed it through your letter box.

MILO.   Er . . . What's this? (Indicating life-size figure of a
sailor sitting in front of window)

ANDREW.   Oh that's Jolly Jack Tar the Jovial Sailor. He and I
have a very good relationship. I make the jokes and he
laughs at them. (He moves the sailor's head manually)
You see ha ha! Now let me get you a drink. (Moves to
drinks trolley) What will you have? Scotch, Gin, Vodka?

MILO.   Scotch.

4

ANDREW. How do you like it? Soda, water, ice?

MILO. Just ice. And what's this?

(MILO has crossed to table downstage left centre on which there is a large game)

ANDREW. Oh that's a game.

MILO. It looks like a child's game. (He picks up one of the pieces)

ANDREW. It's anything but childish I can assure you. I've been studying it for months, and I'm still only a novice. It's called Senat, played by the Ancient Egyptians. It's an early blocking game, not unlike our own Nine Men Morris. Would you mind putting that back where you found it. It's taken me a long time to get it there. How are you settling in at Laundry Cottage?

MILO. Very well.

ANDREW. Using it for weekends, that sort of thing?

MILO. Yes, that's the sort of thing.

ANDREW. It's a charming little place. Well, cheers.

MILO. Cheers.

ANDREW. Now do come and sit down. Forgive me if I just tidy up a bit. I've just reached the denouement of my new book. "The Body On the Tennis Court." Tell me would you agree that the detective story is the normal recreation of noble minds?

MILO. Who said that?

ANDREW. Oh I'm quoting Philip Guedalla. A biographer of the thirties. The golden age when every cabinet minister

5

had a thriller by his bedside, and all the detectives were titled. Before your time I expect.

MILO.   Perhaps it would have been truer to say that noble minds were the normal recreation of detective story writers.

ANDREW.   Yes. Good point. You know even in these days I still set my own work among the gentry. And a great number of people enjoy it, in spite of the Welfare State.

MILO.   I'm surprised they haven't done any of your stuff on television.

ANDREW.   Oh God forbid.

MILO.   Well they're always doing crime stories.

ANDREW.   What—you mean those ghastly things where the police race around in cars and call all the suspects chummy?

MILO.   Yes. That's the kind of thing.

ANDREW.   Oh no that's not my line of country at all. That is detective fact not detective fiction.

MILO.   And of course as such is of much less interest to noble minds.

ANDREW.   Yes, yes you've put it in a nut shell, my dear Milo, if I may so address you.

MILO.   Of course.

ANDREW.   Thank you, we need to be friendly. Now do sit down and let me get you another drink. I'm one up on you already.

(MILO starts to sit in chair below staircase. ANDREW moves to drinks table)

I understand you want to marry my wife.

(A pause. MILO is disconcerted by the directness of the question)

You'll forgive me raising the matter, but as Marguerite is away for a few days, she's up in the North you know visiting some relatives . . .

MILO. Is she?

ANDREW. Yes, so I thought it an appropriate time for a little chat.

MILO. Yes.

ANDREW. Well is it true?

MILO. Well . . . Well, yes, with your permission of course.

ANDREW. Oh yes of course. (He crosses to MILO) Zere, put zat behind your necktie.

MILO. Cheers.

ANDREW. Prosit. (He stands in front of the fireplace) Yes I'm glad to see you're not like so many young men these days seem to think they can do anything they like without asking anyone's permission.

MILO. Certainly not.

ANDREW. Good. I'm pleased to hear it. I know you won't object then if I ask you a few questions about your parents and so on.

MILO. My mother was born in Hereford, a farmer's daughter. My father is an Italian who came to this country in the thirties.

ANDREW. Jewish?

MILO. Half, on his mother's side, that for the Fascists was the important side. The male they felt didn't transmit the disease so virulently.

ANDREW. (tut-tutting) Dreadful business, dreadful.

MILO. Of course I'm not at all religious myself, I'm an agnostic.

ANDREW. (crosses to centre stage) My dear boy, you don't have to explain to me. We're all liberals here. I have no prejudice against Jews, or even half-Jews. Why some of my best friends are half-Jews . . . Mind you I hope you have no objections to any children that you and my wife may have being brought up Church of England?

MILO. None whatsoever if that's what Marguerite wants.

ANDREW. You haven't discussed it yet?

MILO. Not yet, it doesn't seem to have cropped up.

ANDREW. Well I suppose in some ways that's rather a relief. But if you take my advice you'll opt for C of E. It's so much simpler. A couple of hours on Christmas Eve and Good Friday and you've seen the whole thing off nicely. And if you throw in Remembrance Sunday they give you the good Christian medal with oak leaf cluster.

MILO. It's the same with a lot of Jews. My father used to say "most people only talk to their really old friends two or three times a year. Why should God be angry if He gets the same treatment?"

ANDREW.   (insincerely) Very amusing. Your father? Was his
        name Tindle? It doesn't sound very Italian.

MILO.   His name was Tindolini. But if you had a name like
        that in England in those days you had to make a-da-nice
        cream. He was a watch-maker and so he changed it.

ANDREW.   Was he a successful man?

MILO.   No. His business failed. He went back to Italy. I send
        money from time to time and go and visit him and get a
        little sun or ski-ing, depending, of course, on the season.

ANDREW.   Ah!

MILO.   It's not that I'm disloyal to Britain, you understand. It's
        just that the Cairngorms and Minehead don't offer
        quite the same attractions.

ANDREW.   And you? What do you do?

MILO.   I'm in the Travel business. I have my own agency in
        Dulwich.

ANDREW.   Tindle's Travels, eh? I see, and where do you live?

MILO.   I live above the office.

ANDREW.   In Dulwich?

MILO.   Yes, I rent the whole house. It's really most convenient,
        and . . . and it's most attractive, too. It's Georgian.

ANDREW.   H'm. I'm sure it's perfectly delightful but I doubt
        whether an 18th century architectural gem in Dulwich
        whispers quite the same magic to Marguerite as it does to
        you.

MILO.   She adores old houses. She can't wait to live there.

ANDREW.   I understood she was already living there—at least for a couple of nights a week. I'm not mistaken, am I?

(MILO shrugs in embarrassment)

And surely your motive in renting the cottage down here was to increase the incidence of this hebdomadal coupling?

MILO.   I came to be near the woman I love. It is a great pain for us to be apart. You wouldn't understand.

ANDREW.   Possibly. But I understand Marguerite well enough to know that she does not adore old houses. She's lived here quite a time, and between them the rising damp and the Death Watch Beetle have put the boot into her good and proper. She's only got to see a mullioned window and it brings her out in lumps.

MILO.   (hotly) Perhaps it wasn't the house so much as the person she had to share it with.

ANDREW.   Now, now. I thought you were well brought up. Surely you know it's very rude to make personal remarks.

MILO.   I'm sorry. You were disparaging my lover.

ANDREW.   On the contrary, I was reminiscing about my wife.

MILO.   It comes to the same thing.

ANDREW.   Things mostly do, you know. I'll wager that within a year, it's you who will be doing the disparaging, and I who will be doing the rhapsodising, having quite forgotten how intolerably tiresome, vain, spendthrift, self-indulgent and generally bloody crafty she really is.

MILO.   If you don't love Marguerite, you don't have to abuse her.

ANDREW.   Never speak ill of the deadly eh?

MILO.   Now look here . . .

ANDREW.   If I choose to say that my wife converses like a
child of six, cooks like a Brightlingsea landlady, and
makes love like a coelacanth I shall.

MILO.   That's just about enough . . .

ANDREW.   And I certainly don't need her lover's permission to
do so either. In fact, the only thing I need to know from
you is, can you afford to take her off my hands?

MILO.   Afford to . . .

ANDREW.   Afford to support her in the style to which she
wasn't accustomed before she met me, but now is.

(MILO gestures around the room)

MILO.   She won't need all this when we're married. It'll be a
different life—a life of love and simplicity. Now go ahead
—sneer at that. It's almost a national sport in this
country—sneering at love.

ANDREW.   I don't have to sneer at it. I simply don't believe
you. For Marguerite, love is the fawning of a willing lap
dog, and simplicity a square cut 10-carat diamond from
Van Cleef and Arpels.

(MILO rises to his feet, and moves to drinks table to put
down glass)

MILO.   I don't know what I'm doing here. With a little effort
I'm sure you could find a much more appreciative
audience.

ANDREW.   Oh now, Milo. You disappoint me. Rising to your
feet like that and *bridling*.

MILO. (abashed) I wasn't bridling. I was protesting.

ANDREW. It looked like a good old fashioned Hedy Lamarr bridle to me.

MILO. (turning to ANDREW) Who?

ANDREW. Oh very good! Very good! Why don't you just sit down and we'll talk about something that matters desperately to both of us.

MILO. Marguerite?

ANDREW. Money! Have you got any?

MILO. Well I'm not a millionaire, but I've got the lease on the house and some capital equipment, and the turnover in the business this year has been growing every month. By this time next year I . . .

ANDREW. This year, next year, sometime never. What you're saying in fact is that at present you're skint.

MILO. I'll survive.

ANDREW. I'm sure you will but survival is not the point. Presumably when you're married to Marguerite you'll want a fast car, a little place in the sun, and a couple of mistresses.

MILO. Why presumably? Just because you need those things.

ANDREW. Certainly I do. And so does every right thinking insecure, deceitful man. The point is how to get them. (He moves to drinks table)

MILO. I'm sure you do alright. (He crosses to fireplace)

ANDREW. Me? Oh no. Just this fading mansion, the slowest Lagonda in Wiltshire, and only one mistress, I'm afraid.

MILO. Tēa? The Finnish lady who runs the Sauna Bath at Swindon.

ANDREW. Oh, so you know about her, do you?

MILO. Marguerite and I have no secrets from each other.

ANDREW. Not even mine, it seems. (Mock mystical) Tēa is a Karelian Goddess. Her mother was Ilma, supreme divinity of the air; her father was Jumala, the great Creator. Her golden hair smells of pine, and her cobalt eyes are the secret forest pools of Finlandia.

MILO. I hear she's a scrubbed blonde with all the sex appeal of chilled Dettol.

ANDREW. (with dignity) There are those who believe that cleanliness is next to sexiness. And if I were you I wouldn't pay much attention to what Marguerite says. You can take it from me that Tēa's an engaging little trollop, and she suits me mightily. Mind you, she takes a bit of keeping up with, it's a good thing I'm pretty much of an Olympic sexual athlete.

MILO. I suppose these days you're concentrating on the sprints rather than on the long distance stuff.

ANDREW. Not so, dear boy. (He sits) I'm in the pink of condition. I could copulate for England at any distance.

MILO. Well, they do say in Olympic circles, that the point is to take part, rather than to win, so I suppose there's hope for us all. Are you going to marry her?

ANDREW. Marry a Goddess? I wouldn't presume. I might get turned into a birch tree for my audacity. Oh no I simply want to live with her.

MILO. So what's stopping you?

ANDREW. Basically the firm of Prurient and Pry Ltd., whom you and Marguerite have seen fit to employ. Don't look so innocent. Those Woodbine stained private detectives who've been camping outside Tēa's flat for the last week.

MILO. (crossing to centre stage) So you spotted them?

ANDREW. A Bantu with glaucoma couldn't have missed them. No-one can read the Evening News for four hours in a Messerschmidt bubble car, and expect to remain undetected.

MILO. Sorry about that. It was Marguerite's idea.

ANDREW. Who else's? Who paid?

MILO. I did.

ANDREW. I wonder you could afford it.

MILO. It was an insurance policy against you changing your mind about divorcing Marguerite.

ANDREW. My dear boy, let us have no misunderstanding. I've nothing against you marrying Marguerite. There's nothing I want more than to see you two tucked up together. But it's got to be a fixture. I want to be rid of her for life, not just a two week Tindle Tour, economy class. No, you listen to me. You don't know her like I do. You think you do, but you don't. The real truth of the matter is that if you fail her, by which I mean cancelling the account at Harrods, or short-changing her on winter in Jamaica, she'll be back to me in a jiffy mewing for support—and guilty wife or no, she may be entitled to get it.

MILO. Don't be so bloody pathetic. Winter in Jamaica? I'm not going to take her for winter in Jamaica. You're

worrying unnecessarily. Once Marguerite is married to me she'll never think of returning to you. Never. And don't worry about me being able to look after her either.

ANDREW. I see. You mean as soon as you and she are married, Marguerite will joyously exchange Cartiers for the Co-op?

MILO. So she's used to luxury. Whose fault is that?

ANDREW. It's not a fault if you can afford it. But can you? Knowing you to be hard up has she shown any sign of mending her ways in these last idyllic three months? When did she last turn down Bollinger for the blandishments of Baby cham? Or reject Crepes Suzettes in favour of Roly Poly? No, no I'm not joking, how much has this brief liaison cost you so far? £500? £800, £1,000? And that father of yours in Italy, when did you last send him any money? You see why I'm concerned. I tell you. She'll ruin you. To coin a phrase, in two years you'll be a used gourd. And what's more, a used gourd with a sizeable overdraft.

MILO. We've often talked about money. I've told her we spend too much.

ANDREW. And she takes no notice?

MILO. (low) None.

ANDREW. A silvery laugh? A coquettish turn of the head?

MILO. Something like that.

ANDREW. Exactly. Well, it's to solve this little problem that I have invited you here tonight. This, as they say, is where the plot thickens.

MILO. Ah!

2   15

ANDREW.   I'll get you another drink.

(He crosses to drinks table. In "Listen with Mother" style)

Are you sitting comfortably? Then I'll begin. Once upon a time there was an Englishman called Andrew Wyke who, in common with most of his countrymen was virtually castrated by taxation. To avoid total emasculation, his accountants advised him, just before the last devaluation, to put a considerable part of his money, some £135,000, into jewellery. His wife, of course, was delighted.

MILO.   You made her a present of it?

ANDREW.   Absolutely not. It's still mine, as well she knows. But we felt she might as well wear it, as bank it. After all, it's fully insured.

MILO.   I see what you mean by the plot thickening. It usually does when insurance is mentioned.

ANDREW.   I'm glad you follow me so readily. I want you to steal that jewellery.

MILO.   (astounded) What?

ANDREW.   Tonight, for choice. Marguerite is out of the house. It's an admirable opportunity.

MILO.   You must be joking.

ANDREW.   You would know it if I were.

MILO.   (playing for time) But . . . But what about the servants?

ANDREW.   I've sent Mr. and Mrs. Hawkins to
Weston-super-Mare for a 48 hour paddle. They won't be
back till Sunday night. So, the house is empty.

MILO.   I see.

ANDREW.   What do you say?

MILO.   It sounds criminal.

ANDREW.   Of course it's criminal. All good money-making
schemes in England have got to be these days. The
jewellery, when it's not in the bank, lives in the safe
under the stairs. It's there now. All you have to do is steal
them, and sell them abroad and live happily ever after
with Marguerite. All I have to do is to claim the
insurance money and live happily ever after with Tēa.
(Pause) Well, in my case perhaps, not ever after, but at
least until I get fed up with a cuisine based on the elk.

MILO.   Is that what you asked me over to hear? A scummy
little plot to defraud the insurance company?

ANDREW.   I'm sorry you find the plot scummy. I thought it
was nicely clear and simple.

MILO.   Nicely obvious and clearly unworkable. Supposing I do
as you say and take the jewels. If I sell them to a fence,
always supposing I could find one, I'd get a fraction of
their value.

ANDREW.   Not with the fences I know.

MILO.   (derisory) What fences would you know?

ANDREW.   I know some of the finest fences in Europe.
Prudent yet prodigal. I met them some years ago while
researching "The Deadly Affair of the Druce Diamond."

MILO.   Never read it.

17

ANDREW.   You never read it! I suppose you're going to tell me
you never read "Diet of Worms," or "The Mystery of the
Plantaganet Parakeet?"

MILO.   Sorry.

ANDREW.   Haven't you read any of my books?

MILO.   I'm afraid not. What were you telling me about fences?

ANDREW.   That I know a great many. In fact on your behalf
I have already contacted a certain gentleman in
Amsterdam. He will treat you very well; you won't get
full value of the jewels but you will get two-thirds, say
£90,000, and you'll get it in cash.

MILO.   Why should this man be so generous?

ANDREW.   Because he will have what fences never have—title
to the jewels. I will see to it that in addition to the
jewels, you also steal the receipts I got for them. All you
have to do is hand them over together. Now what does
my Insurance Company discover when it swings into
action, antennae pulsing with suspicion? It discovers
that someone impersonating Andrew Wyke sold the
jewels for £90,000 cash. They've still got to pay me.
Hard cheese. Think it over. Take your time. There's no
hurry.

(A pause. MILO considers the proposition. ANDREW
walks away from MILO, humming lightly to himself. He
stops by a roll-a-penny wall game and plays to a successful
conclusion. MILO paces up and down, indecisive. He
suddenly turns and faces ANDREW)

MILO.   Look, I know this sounds stupid, but . . . but well, have
you had any experience—I mean, have you ever actually
committed a crime before?

ANDREW.   Only in the mind's eye, so to speak. For the

purpose of my books. St. John Lord Merridew would have a pretty lean time of it if I didn't give him any crime to solve.

MILO.   Who?

ANDREW.   My detective, St. John Lord Merridew. Known to millions all over the civilized world. "An ambulatory tun of port with the face of Father Christmas." That's how I describe him. "A classical scholar with a taste for good pipes and bad puns, but with a nose for smelling out evil, superior to anything, in the force."

MILO.   Oh yes, the police are always stupid in your kind of story, aren't they? They never solve anything. Only an amateur sleuth ever knows what's happening. But that is detective fiction. This is fact.

ANDREW.   I am aware of the difference, Milo. I also know that insurance investigators are sharp as razors, and that's why, as they say in the Athenaeum, everything's got to be done Kosher and according to cocker.

MILO.   I'm just saying there's a difference between writing and real life, that's all. And there's another thing. How do I know this thing isn't one big frame up?

ANDREW.   Frame up?

MILO.   Yes. That you really hate my association with your wife and would give five years of Olympian sexual athleticism to see me in jail. Once I'm clear of the house, an anonymous 'phone call to the police . . .

ANDREW.   And be stuck with Marguerite for another bickering eternity? Bodystockings on the breakfast tray, false eyelashes in the wash basin, the bottles, the lotions, the unguents, the oils, the tribal record player and that ceaseless vapid yak. Oh yes, I could shop you to the police, nothing easier, but whatever for. Still, it's for you to evaluate, old boy.

MILO. Well I . . . I er . . .

ANDREW. If you don't trust me . . .

MILO. Oh, I trust you but . . .

ANDREW. It's a very simple proposition. You have an expensive woman and no money. It seems to me if you want to keep Marguerite there is only one thing you can do—you must steal those jewels.

MILO. Why don't *you* steal them and simply hand them over to me?

ANDREW. I should have thought that was obvious. The burglary has to look real. The house has actually to be broken into.

MILO. Well, why don't *you* break into it?

ANDREW. (Brooklyn accent) Hey, Milo baby, will you do me a favour. Leave this to me, huh? You know what I mean? Crime is my specialty. I've got such a great plan and I've got it all worked out to the last detail. You're the star, I'm just the producer.

MILO. £90,000?

ANDREW. (deliberately) £90,000 tax free. In cash. It would take a lot of Tindle Tours to make that kind of money. (they laugh together. MILO is convinced)

MILO. Alright, I'll do it. Where shall I break in? (MILO rushes for the stairs)

ANDREW. Hold your horses. Now the first thing you've got to do is disguise yourself.

MILO.   What on earth for?

ANDREW.   Supposing someone saw you climbing in.

MILO.   Who? You're not overlooked.

ANDREW.   Who knows? A dallying couple. A passing sheep
rapist. And, dear boy, remember the clues we're to leave
for the police and the Insurance Company. We don't
want your footsteps in the flowerbeds, or your coat button
snagged on the window-sill. Oh no, you must be
disguised.

MILO.   Alright, what do you suggest?

ANDREW.   (ANDREW crosses to upstage left and brings a
large hamper to downstage left) As Marguerite has
assuredly told you, in younger days we were always
dressing up in this house. What with amateur dramatics,
and masquerades and costume balls, there was virtually
no end to the concealment of identity.

MILO.   She's never mentioned it.

ANDREW.   No . . . ? (a touch wistful) Well, it was all some
years ago. (briskly) Anyway, let's see what we've got. (He
opens the basket. He holds up the pieces of the burglar
suit one by one and puts them on MILO.) Item. A face
mask, a flat cap, a striped jersey and bag marked Swag.

MILO.   I thought the idea was that I was *not* to be taken as
a burglar.

ANDREW.   Fashions have changed you know.

MILO.   Not quickly enough. It's asking for trouble.

(ANDREW puts the costume back and brings out a Ku
Klux Klan outfit)

ANDREW. Ku Klux Klan invade country home. Fiery cross, flames on Salisbury plain. Police baffled.

MILO. Isn't it a trifle conspicuous for Wiltshire?

ANDREW. Yes, you may be right! (ANDREW holds up a monk's costume) Here is one of my favourites. How about Brother Lightfingers?

MILO. Oh, for God's sake . . .

(MILO shakes his head decisively)

ANDREW. Oh, come on. Let's make this a Gothic folly. (Jesuit priest voice) Perhaps we shall never know the identity of the cowled figure seen haunting the grounds of the Manor House on the night of the terrible murder. Even today, some locals claim to hear the agonised screams of the victim echoing around the chimney pots.

MILO. Murder? Anguished screams of the victim? What are you talking about? It's a simple robbery we're staging here, that's all.

(An uneasy pause)

ANDREW. (normal voice) Quite right, Milo. I was carried away for a moment. I'm not sure I wasn't going to add a crucified countess entombed in her bedroom, guarded by a man eating sparrow-hawk.

MILO. Look here, Andrew, you probably think this is one huge joke. But it's my freedom you're playing with.

ANDREW. I'm merely trying to bring a little romance into modern crime, and incidentally into your life.

MILO. Marguerite will bring all the romance into my life I need, thank you all the same.

ANDREW. Marguerite romantic? Marguerite couldn't have got Johann Strauss to waltz.

MILO. Look, Andrew, these are great costumes, but haven't you just got an old pair of wellies, a raincoat and a sock that I can pull over my head?

ANDREW. Old pair of wellies and a sock? How dreary! That's the whole trouble with crime today. No imagination. I mean you tell me, does your heart beat any faster when you hear that a lorry load of cigarettes has been knocked off in the Walworth Road?

MILO. Not particularly.

ANDREW. Well of course not. Or that a 93 year old night watchman has had his silly interfering old skull split open with a lead pipe?

MILO. Of course not.

ANDREW. Well then, what's the matter with you? Where's your spunk? Let's give our crime the true sparkle of the thirties, a little amateur aristocratic quirkiness. Think of all that wonderful material. There's the ice dagger, the poison that leaves no trace, the Regie cigarette stubbed in the ash tray, charred violet note paper in the grate, Dusenberg tyre marks in the drive way, the gramophone record simulating conversation, the clutching hand from behind the arras, sinister orientals, twin brothers from Australia, "hi there cobber, hi there blue," where were you on the night of the 13th? I swear I didn't do it, Inspector, I'm innocent I tell you, innocent . . .

MILO. God you've gone off like a fire-cracker!

ANDREW. And why not? We're on the brink of a great crime. Don't you feel the need to give your old archenemy Inspector Plodder of the Yard a run for his money? And you're the Star, you're the who-what-dun-it!

MILO.   Well what about this? (He holds up Courtier's costume)

ANDREW.   Ah! Monsieur Beaucaire. He's very good. Lots of beauty spots and wig powder to let fall all over the place. Or what about this? Little Bo Peep?

(ANDREW sings Little Bo Peep and dances about holding up the costume)

MILO.   No.

ANDREW.   Why not?

MILO.   I haven't got the figure for it.

ANDREW.   Are you quite sure? An indifferent figure shouldn't materially affect the execution of this crime.

MILO.   Quite sure.

ANDREW.   Well you are choosey, aren't you? There's not a great deal left.

(He pulls out a Clown's costume. Large pantaloons, waiter's dicky, tail coat)

We'll have to settle for Joey.

MILO.   Wow!

ANDREW.   Can't you see it all, the tinsel, the glitter, the lights, the liberty horses, the roar of the crowd, and Milo all the kiddies love you.

MILO.   (happily) Alright! It seems the costume most appropriate to this scheme.

ANDREW.   Well give me your coat I'll hang it up for you. We don't want the police to find any fibres of this beautiful suit.

24

(MILO takes off his jacket and gives it to ANDREW)

Oh and the shirt and trousers too.

MILO. What?

ANDREW. Oh yes, you know how clever they are in those
laboratories of theirs. That's it. Don't be shy. Into your
smalls. Oh I know a well brought up boy when I see one.
Folds his pants at night.

(MILO gives him his carefully folded trousers.
ANDREW runs up the stairs and with a sudden violent
gesture, roughly throws the suit in the wardrobe, while
MILO takes off his shirt and tie and shoes)

MILO. Shirt and shoes.

(MILO holds up his shirt, shoes and tie)

ANDREW. Very good, sir. The Quick Clean Valet Service
always at your disposal, sir.

(He pushes them into the wardrobe, then watches MILO
changing with great satisfaction)

(softly) Give a clown your finger and he'll take your
hand.

MILO. What was that?

ANDREW. Just an old English Proverb I was thinking of.

(MILO sings to himself "On With the Motley" and
ends it with "£90,000 tax free, in cash" as he dresses)

MILO. Ecco, Milo!

ANDREW. Bravissimo! Now all you need are the boots.

(MILO pulls a huge pair of boots from the basket)

MILO.   Hey I could go skiing on these when I go to Italy.

ANDREW.   The clown is such a happy chap,
His nose is painted red,
His trousers baggy as can be,
A topper on his head.
He jumps around the circus ring,
And juggles for his bread,
Then comes the day he tries a trick,
And drops down . . .

Come on do us a trick.

MILO.   What sort of trick?

ANDREW.   Oh I don't know. Trip up—fall on your arse.

MILO.   Certainly not, I don't think that's a very good idea.

ANDREW.   Well what about a bit of juggling then.

(ANDREW takes two oranges from the drinks table and
throws them to MILO. He then produces an umbrella
from the basket and throws it to MILO who opens it and
runs about the room and finally trips up on his boots)

MILO.   Christ!

ANDREW.   Sorry, dear boy. But you know the rule of the
circus. If at first you don't succeed . . .

MILO.   Give up. Can we get on with this charade, please!

ANDREW.   Of course. Yours to command. (He opens swag
bag) Here are the tools of your trade. One glass cutter to
break in with; a piece of putty for holding on to the cut
piece of glass so it doesn't clatter onto the floor and

awake the ravenous Doberman Pinscher you suspect lurks inside; and a stethoscope.

MILO.   A stethoscope?

ANDREW.   Safe breakers for the use of. The theory is you tried to pick the lock by listening to the tumblers, failed, and then employed gelignite.

MILO.   (alarmed) Gelignite? I don't know anything about gelignite.

ANDREW.   I do. Leave that to me. Now what we want is some supreme bizarre touch to crown the whole edifice—say a signed photograph of Grock left impaled on a splinter of glass.

MILO.   A signed photograph of Grock. (angry) Why don't you take a full page ad in The Times and tell them what we're doing.

ANDREW.   I was only trying to lighten Inspector Plodder's day for him . . . If you don't like the idea . . .

MILO.   (earnestly) There's no such animal as Inspector Plodder outside of books. It'll be Inspector Early Bird, or Superintendent No Stone Unturned. You can bet your bottom dollar on that. And I can't walk in this costume. These boots are ridiculous. (He stumbles and starts to take them off)

ANDREW.   Keep them on. Can't you see it all. Wiltshire paralysed. The West Country in a ferment. Where will Big Boot strike next?

MILO.   But . . .

ANDREW.   (reasonably) All these boots will tell the police is that a true professional realised the flower beds would carry footprints, and decided to disguise his own perhaps a trifle eccentrically. Now are you ready? Got everything? Glass cutter? Putty?

ANDREW.)
MILO.   )   The mask!

(ANDREW takes top hat and mask from basket)

ANDREW.   Good. Now go through that door, round the house and across the lawn. To your right you will discover a shed. In it is a ladder. Bring the ladder back and stand it against the house so you can break in at the gallery.

MILO.   Will you come out and hold it steady?

ANDREW.   Certainly not. I don't want my footprints in the flower beds.

MILO.   I'm not very good at heights.

ANDREW.   Improvise, ducky. Place one foot above the other. It's called climbing.

MILO.   OK.

ANDREW.   Good luck.

(MILO bows and goes through the hall door. ANDREW takes a length of flex and black box with gelignite, black tape and detonator from desk drawer. After a few minutes MILO appears at window upstage left)

ANDREW.   (pause) For Christ's sake can't you keep those bloody boots off my Busy Lizzies.

(MILO disappears and presently reappears with the ladder which he places against the window and starts to climb. ANDREW sits with his back to the window and reacts to the noises he hears. As he attaches the detonator to the flex he speaks in an old woman's voice)

Puss, Puss, Puss, do you hear a noise Puss! Was that a step on the stairs. No, it was just the wind. You know Puss I sometimes think there's a curse on this house. But you shouldn't pay any attention to me. I'm just a silly old woman who is afraid of her own shadow. (noise of glass cutter scoring window) What was that Puss? Someone's prowling in the grounds. We're all going to be murdered in our beds. No, no, the front door's locked, and the window's too high, no one can get into our snug little home.

(MILO drops pane of glass)

(exasperated) What *are* you doing now?

MILO.   I dropped the glass.

(ANDREW groans theatrically. After a further struggle MILO succeeds in climbing through the window, onto the gallery)

Whew! What do I do with the putty?

(He indicates the putty)

ANDREW.   (irritated) Stick it on the wall.

MILO.   I can lose this at any rate. (puts mask on bureau) Now for the safe!

ANDREW.   No. Not straight away. You're not meant to know where they are. Search around. Go into the bedroom. Disturb a few things. Throw some clothes on the floor—Marguerite's for choice . . . That's it.

(MILO goes into the bedroom and returns with a pile of women's clothes which he puts neatly on the floor)

Don't pack 'em. Ravage 'em. Don't you know how burglars leave a place?

(ANDREW takes a flying kick at the pile of his wife's clothes—sending them flying all over the room)

Now try the wardrobe. Rumple the contents a little. Actually that's enough. Those shirts were made for me by Baget & Grub, chemise makers to monarchs.

(MILO throws the shirts out with relish)

MILO.   Got to be thorough. It would be suspicious if the burglar played favourites.

(ANDREW's socks and underwear follow, cascading out all over the gallery)

ANDREW.   Oh, it's a martyrdom. (shouting) Will you stop that, Milo, and rifle that bureau immediately.

(Reluctantly MILO crosses to the bureau and tries a drawer)

MILO.   It's locked.

ANDREW.   Of course it's bloody locked! Use your jemmy on it.

MILO.   I haven't got a jemmy. You didn't give me one.

ANDREW.   (exasperated) Well, we'd better go and find one, hadn't we?

(They tramp downstairs)

30

Honestly, Milo, you are the soppiest night interloper I've ever met. I can't think what Marguerite sees in you.

MILO.   The sympathy and kindness of a kindred spirit, actually.

ANDREW.   It's like a Bengali tiger lying down with a Bush Baby.

MILO.   I know we're a damn sight happier than you are with your ice maiden.

ANDREW.   You probably take it more seriously, that's all.

MILO.   You have to be serious if you want to be in love.

ANDREW.   You have to be serious about crime if you want to afford to be in love. Now get cracking on that bureau.

(MILO climbs the stairs. He starts work on the bureau with the jemmy. After a pause the drawer yields and he opens it)

MILO.   There is a set of false teeth here. They look like a man's.

ANDREW.   (furious) Put them back at once.

MILO.   Sorry. Your spares?

ANDREW.   (pause) Come down at once.

(MILO comes down the stairs and crosses to ANDREW who has plugged the flex into a light switch upstage left)

Keep your feet off the flex. Right, stand by for count down 5—4—3—2—1. Contact!

(Noise of explosion and puff of smoke from safe)

MILO.   There she blows. Ah! It's hot.

ANDREW.   You've got gloves on!—Get in there!
>(MILO rummages in the safe and finds a large jewel box.
>He examines it carefully, occasionally shaking it gently)

What the hell are you shaking it for? It's a jewel box, not
a maraca.

MILO.   I thought it might have some secret catch on it. It's
locked, you see.

ANDREW.   Well, smash it open. Jesus! You've all the killer
instinct of a twenty year old Sealyham.

>(MILO attacks the box with his jemmy)

MILO.   It's such a pretty box—it seems such a waste.

>(The box opens to reveal its precious contents. MILO
>stands entranced letting the jewels flash and sparkle
>through his fingers)

Dear God!

ANDREW.   Ah! Moses looks upon the promised land.

>(MILO sits at base of stairs)

MILO.   They're very beautiful. Look at this ruby necklace?

ANDREW.   That we got on our honeymoon.

MILO.   It's fantastic.

ANDREW.   I never cared for it myself. I always thought it
made Marguerite look like a blood sacrifice.

MILO.   I'd like my father to be here now. Poor blighter, he had
no idea what it was all about . . . sitting there every
night hunched up over those watches like a little old

gnome, squinting his eyesight away, and for what—to give me an education at a second-rate public school. I suppose he thought he had to do it—that he owed it to me and the brave new Anglo-Saxon world he'd adopted. Poor old bugger.

ANDREW. Here, put them in your pocket for a start. I'll get you the receipts in a moment. Now! This is the fun bit. It's the moment when the householder, his attention attracted by the sound of the explosion, surprises his burglar. In the ensuing struggle, the house is sacked.

MILO. Why is it necessary for you to surprise me at all?

ANDREW. Because if I've seen you at close quarters, I can always describe you to the police . . .

(MILO reacts as if hit)

MILO. Now look here . . .

ANDREW. . . . wrongly. (INSPECTOR's voice) Did you manage to get a good look at the intruder's face, sir? (normal voice) Yes, Inspector, I did. It may just have been a trick of the light, but his face didn't look wholly human. If you can imagine a kind of prognathic stoat, fringed about with lilac coloured hair, and seemingly covered in a sort of boot polish . . .

MILO. (patiently) I understand. How much sacking do you want done?

ANDREW. A decent bit, I think, a few chairs on their backs, some china ornaments put to the sword. You know— convincing but not Carthaginian.

(MILO carefully turns a chair over and leans a small table against the sofa. He takes a china ornament and stands it upright on the floor. ANDREW watches impatiently)

Surely you don't call that convincing?

(ANDREW throws over another table, spills the contents of a drawer, and turns books out of his bookcase)

That's better. Let the encyclopaedias fly like autumn leaves. Let the contents of the drawers be scattered to the four winds!

(MILO throws papers into the air in a great cloud)

Ah! A super snowstorm. That's very good. We'll let my accountants sort that lot out later. You know I never liked Saltglaze. I can't think why Marguerite is devoted to it. (He picks a china ornament off the mantelpiece and hurls it across the room) Oh it's coming along nicely, but it still doesn't look right. Come on, let's see what accident does to artifice. (ANDREW seizes MILO and wrestles him round the room, overturning things as they go. MILO, apart from being the shorter, is much hampered by his big boots and floppy clown's clothing, so that ANDREW is able to pummel him severely)

MILO.   You're bigger than I am. It's not fair.

ANDREW.   Nonsense. You're the underdog, aren't you? You've got the support of the crowd.

MILO.   A good big 'un will always lick a good little 'un.

ANDREW.   The bigger they are the harder they fall.

(MILO receives a particularly hard blow)

MILO.   Here, steady on, old man!

ANDREW.   They never come back. (He pushes MILO over the fender into the fireplace)

34

MILO.   Christ! That hurt!

(ANDREW helps him up)

ANDREW.   Come on, back into the ring. Don't despair. This
fight is fixed. It's about now that I take a dive.
This is where you lay me out cold.

MILO.   What? For real?

ANDREW.   Naturally. When the police come I must be able
to show them a real bump.

(MILO smiles weakly)

I thought you'd like this bit.

(MILO tentatively moves towards a lamp)

MILO.   What shall I use?

ANDREW.   Not my opaline if you don't mind.

(MILO picks up the brass poker)

MILO.   This is it. The poker, the original blunt instrument. (He
beats logs viciously)

(ANDREW eyes the poker apprehensively)

ANDREW.   Steady on, Milo. Don't get carried away.

MILO.   Well, I'm doing my best.

ANDREW.   We are not talking about a murder weapon. We
are discussing an object from which I receive, in the
classic formula, a glancing blow which renders me
temporarily unconscious.

MILO.   Such as?

ANDREW.   Well I don't know exactly . . . Frankly I'm rather off this blow business now I've seen you in action. Perhaps we could think of a device which will raise a lump without actually cracking the cranium. Yes, that's it. Now what would those fathers of the scientific detective story, R. Austin Freeman, or Arthur B. Reeve have come up with?

MILO.   Huh?

ANDREW.   You know. The Red Thumb Mark 1907. The Silent Bullet 1912.

MILO.   (trapped into joining in) How about a bee sting projected into the scalp with a blow pipe.

ANDREW.   Oh, Milo, that's absolutely brilliant. Do you have such sting, pipe, or bee?

MILO.   Well . . . no.

ANDREW.   No. Still seven out of ten for trying. I know, you can always tie me up and gag me and leave me to be found by the cleaning woman. (CHARLADY's voice) Lawks, Mr. Wyke, what are you doing all trussed up like a turkey cock?

(ANDREW mimes being tied up and gagged and trying to get the CHARLADY to untie him)

Mmmmmmmmmmmmmm . . . Mmmmmmmmmmmm . . . Mmmmmmmmmmmmmm . . . (CHARLADY's voice) Trying out something for one of them creepy books of yours, are you, sir? Well, don't mind me. I won't disturb you. I'll just get on with my dusting.

MILO.   (patiently) If I don't knock you out, how do I manage to tie you up?

36

ANDREW. (normal voice) That's a very good question. I know. You could hold a gun on me.

MILO. We professional burglars don't like firearms much.

ANDREW. But, as you're a rank amateur you can conquer your scruples.

(ANDREW produces a gun from the desk drawer)

Here. How about this? Don't you think its wicked looking blue barrel is just the thing.

MILO. Is it loaded?

ANDREW. Naturally. What use would it be otherwise? And I think it should go off a couple of times in the struggle.

MILO. Why?

ANDREW. It would add credence to my story of your holding a gun on me. Hearing a noise and fearing burglars, I took my revolver and went to investigate. You attacked me. In the struggle it went off. Being an old fraidy cat householder, I allowed brutish you to take possession of it. You then held it on me while you tied me up. Right?

MILO. I suppose so.

ANDREW. Uninventive but believable. Now then, what to sacrifice? What do you say to the demolition of that gaudy Swansea puzzle jug? The gloriously witty idea is that when you tip it up the liquid pours out of a hole in the back, and not through the spout.

MILO. A bit obvious, really.

ANDREW. Exactly! Obvious and ugly. Let us expose its shortcomings.

(ANDREW draws a bead on it, then lowers the gun)

On the other hand, the creme brule colouring lends it an attractive solidity I should miss. Now how about that giant Staffordshire mug with the inscription on it? What does it say?

(MILO moves a little towards it and reads it out)

MILO. (reading) In the real cabinet of friendship everyone helped his neighbour and said to his brother be of good cheer.

ANDREW. Proletarian pomposity!

(ANDREW suddenly raises his gun and fires, shattering the jug. MILO turns in surprise, as he realises the bullet must have passed reasonably close to his head)

You might have said good shot.

MILO. Good shot.

ANDREW. (insouciant) It's nothing.

(ANDREW looks around him. His eye falls on a china figurine poised on the banister rail above him. He takes aim)

Down with all deviationist, reactionary Dresden Shepherdesses.

(He shoots and the Dresden Shepherdess flies into pieces)

MILO. Bravo!

ANDREW. What fun this is! Did you ever know Charlie Begby?

MILO. I don't think so.

ANDREW. Terribly funny fellow. I once saw him bag three brace of duck with one shot.

MILO. No!

ANDREW. Yes. Three brace with one shot! The only trouble was, they were china ducks on his aunty's drawing room wall. I said "oh Charlie you can't do that, it's the close season." (He presses a button on the desk and the sailor laughs) I told you, he always laughs at my jokes.

(MILO laughs. ANDREW's mood changes abruptly)

It's not really all that funny. There's an open season on some creatures all the year round.

(ANDREW turns the gun on MILO)

Seducers and wife stealers for example.

MILO. (nervous) Only in Italian opera surely.

ANDREW. (hard) You should know. It's your country of origin, is it not?

MILO. No. I was actually born here in England.

ANDREW. Were you now. Dear old cradle-of-the-parliamentary-system-who-screws-my-wife-merits-a-large-pink-gin-England?

MILO. Sense-of-humour-fair-trail-England, I mean.

ANDREW. That's the way a foreigner talks. In private he thinks, filthy wet country, ugly red cold men who don't know how to treat women.

39

MILO.   What's brought all this on? What are you doing with
        that gun?

ANDREW.   Pretty obviously pointing it at you.

MILO.   For God's sake, why?

ANDREW.   (slowly, Italian accent) Because I'm going to kill
        you.

MILO.   You're going to . . . (laughs nervously) Oh Jesus! I
        suppose this is some sort of game.

ANDREW.   Yes. We've been playing it all evening. It's called
        "You're going to die and no-one will suspect murder."

        (A pause. MILO considers his position)

MILO.   You mean all this steal my wife's jewels stuff was
        just a . . .

ANDREW.   Of course! I invited you here to set up the
        circumstances of your own death. The break in, the
        disguise, the jewels in your pocket, the householder
        aroused, the gun going off in the struggle and then the
        final fatal shot. I might even get a commendation from
        the police, for "having a go."

MILO.   For God's sake, Andrew, knock it off!

ANDREW.   Can you find a flaw in it?

MILO.   (beginning to feel desperate) Marguerite! They'll trace
        the connection between me and Marguerite. They'll
        know that's why you did it.

ANDREW.   I am quite entitled to tackle a man wearing a mask
        plundering my house in the middle of the night. How
        was I expected to know who you were? Oh no, the law

will have every sympathy with me. Property has always
been more highly regarded than people in England. Even
Marguerite will assume you were just an adventurer who
only loved her for her jewels—a petty sneak thief who
found larceny less burdensome than marriage. You really
are a dead duck, aren't you? Not a moral or romantic
attitude left.

MILO.   I believe you *are* serious.

ANDREW.   I'm not afraid of killing you, if that's what you
mean.

MILO.   You've got to be. Mortally afraid for your soul.

ANDREW.   I didn't think the Jews believed in hell.

MILO.   We believe in not playing games with life.

ANDREW.   Ha! Wit in the face of adversity. You've learnt
something from the English. Well here's something else
to learn. A sporting chance. Why don't you run for it?

MILO.   And give you the chance to shoot me down in cold
blood?

ANDREW.   In hot blood you mean. I'm going to shoot you
down in cold blood anyway.

(MILO tries to run but falls over his boots)

MILO.   Look, stop pointing that gun at me . . . I hate guns
. . . please . . . this is sick.

ANDREW.   You should be flattered by the honour I'm doing
you—to take your life lightheartedly—to make your death
the centre piece of an arranged bit of fun. To put it
another way, your demise will recreate a noble mind.

MILO.   This is where I came in.

ANDREW. And where you go out, I'm afraid. The only
question to be decided is where the police shall find you.
Sprawled over the desk like countless colonels in
countless studies? Or propped up in the log basket like a
rag doll? Which do you think? Early Agatha Christie or
middle Nicholas Blake?

MILO. For Christ's sake, Andrew, this is not a detective story,
this is real life. You are talking of doing a real murder. Of
killing a real man—don't you understand?

ANDREW. Perhaps I shouldn't do it with a gun at all. Perhaps
I should shove the ham knife into you, and leave you face
down in the middle of the room—(melodramatic
voice)—your blood staining the flagstones a deep
carmine.

(MILO shudders)

MILO. Oh God!

ANDREW. Or best of all, how about a real 1930's murder
weapon—the mashie niblick. I've got one in my golf bag.

(ANDREW fetches the golf club from the hall. MILO
dives for the telephone but is too late)

You would be discovered in the fireplace, I think in a fair
old mess. (dramatic voice) The body lay on its back, its
limbs grotesquely splayed like a broken puppet. The
whole head had been pulped as if by some superhuman
force. (INSPECTOR's voice) "My God" breathed the
Inspector, blenching. "Thompson, you'd better get a
tarpaulin . . . Excuse me sir, but was all this violence
strictly necessary?" (own voice) I'm sorry Inspector. It
was when I saw him handling my wife's nightdresses. I
must have completely lost control of myself.
(INSPECTOR's voice) "That's quite alright sir. Don't
get excited. I quite understand." (ANDREW throws
down golf club) No. I don't like it. I think the scene the

police find is simply this. After the fight you flee up the
stairs to regain your ladder. I catch you on the landing
and in the renewed struggle I shoot you. Nothing
succeeds like simplicity, don't you agree, Milo? Now
then, some of my own finger prints on my own revolver.
(ANDREW takes his glove off and holds the gun in his
naked hand) On your feet, up!

(ANDREW forces MILO to mount the stairs by shoving
the gun in his back. MILO gives a sudden spasmodic
shudder)

Did you know that Charles I put on two shirts the
morning of his execution? "If I tremble with cold," he
said, "my enemies will say it was from fear; I will not
expose myself to such reproaches." You must also
attempt dignity as you mount the steps to the scaffold.

(MILO demurs and sinks to his knees near the top step)

MILO.   (terrified and pleading) But why, Andrew? Why?

ANDREW.   Don't snivel. You can't think it'll gain you mercy.

MILO.   I must know why!

ANDREW.   I'm amazed you have to ask. But since you do, it's
    perfectly simple. I hate you. I hate your smarmy, good
    looking Latin face and your easy manner. I'll bet you're
    easy in a ski lodge, and easy on a yacht, and easy on a
    beach. I'll bet you a pound to a penny, that you wear
    a gold charm round your neck, and that your chest is
    hairy and in summer matted with sun oil. I hate you
    because you are a mock humble, jewelled, shot cuff-link
    sponger, a world is my oysterer, a seducer of silly women,
    and a king among marshmallow snakes. I hate you
    because you are a culling spick. A wop—a not one of me.
    Come, little man, did you really believe I would give up
    my wife and jewels to you? That I would make myself
    that ridiculous?

MILO. Why not? You're not in love with her.

ANDREW. She's mine whether I love her or not. I found
her, I've kept her. I am familiar with her.
And once, she was in love with me.

MILO. And now she's in love with me, and the dog in the
manger won't let go. (tries to attack him) The mad
dog in the manger who should be put down for everyone's
sake.

ANDREW. (deadly) And you are a young man, dressed as
a clown about to be murdered. Put the mask on, Milo.
(a pause)

MILO. No please.

(ANDREW reaches up and lifts the clown mask off the
newel post)

ANDREW. Put it on!

(MILO takes the mask and fumbles it onto his face)

Excellent. Farewell Punchinello!

(ANDREW lifts the pistol to MILO's head. MILO is
shaking with fear)

MILO. (high falsetto) Please . . .
(ANDREW slowly pulls the trigger. MILO falls
backwards down the stairs and lies still. ANDREW walks
past him, pausing to peer closely to see whether there is
any sign of life. He lifts the lolling head and lets it thump
back, carelessly, onto the stairs. Satisfied that he has done
his work well, he straightens up, and smiles to himself)

ANDREW. Game and set, I believe.

Slow Curtain

44

ACT TWO

(The curtain rises to the sound of the slow movement of
Beethoven's Seventh Symphony which is playing on a
record player. ANDREW enters from kitchen with a tray
containing a large pot of caviare, toast, wedge of lemon, a
bottle of champagne and glass. He puts tray on desk and
stands conducting the music. The Movement comes to
an end. ANDREW crosses to record player and turns
over the record. He returns to desk and starts to eat.

The telephone rings)

ANDREW.   Hullo . . . Yes, Hawkins, where are you? What?
Well, you should have checked the times of the trains
. . . I've had to get my own supper for the third time
running . . . Yes, yes, I daresay, but you know how
helpless I am without you and Mrs. H. Man cannot live
on Baked Beans alone, you know . . . Alright . . .
Alright, tomorrow morning. But first thing, mind you.

(ANDREW continues eating for some moments. The
front doorbell rings. After a slight pause ANDREW goes
to answer it)

DOPPLER.   (offstage in hall) Good evening, sir.

ANDREW.   Evening.

DOPPLER.   Mr. Wyke.

ANDREW.   Yes?

46

DOPPLER. My name is Inspector Doppler, sir. Detective
Inspector Doppler. Of the Wiltshire County
Constabulary. I'm sorry to be calling so late. May I have
a few words with you on a very important matter?

(ANDREW enters, followed by INSPECTOR
DOPPLER, a heavily built, tallish man of about 50. His
hair is balding, and he wears cheap round spectacles on
his fleshy nose, above a greying moustache. His clothes,
dark rumpled suit, under a half-open light coloured
mackintosh occasion no surprise, nor does his pork pie
hat)

ANDREW. The Wiltshire County Constabulary you say?
(turning off music) Come in. Always pleased to see the
police.

DOPPLER. Can't say the same about everyone, sir. Most
people seem to have what you might call an allergy to us.

ANDREW. Would you join me in a brandy, Inspector? Or are
you going to tell me you don't drink on duty?

DOPPLER. Oh no, sir. I always drink on duty. I can't afford to
in my own time.

(DOPPLER sits centre)

ANDREW. (handing the INSPECTOR a brandy) Well, what
can I do for you, Inspector?

DOPPLER. I'm investigating a disappearance, sir.

ANDREW. Disappearance?

DOPPLER. Yes, sir. Of a Mr. Milo Tindle. Do you know him,
sir?

ANDREW. Yes, that's the chap who's taken Laundry Cottage.

47

DOPPLER. He walked out of his cottage on Friday night and hasn't been seen since.

ANDREW. Great Scott.

DOPPLER. Do you know this gentleman well, sir?

ANDREW. Vaguely. He came to the house once or twice. How can I help you?

DOPPLER. When did you last see Mr. Tindle, sir?

ANDREW. Oh, months ago. I can't exactly remember. As I told you, he wasn't a close friend; rather more an acquaintance.

DOPPLER. Really, sir. That doesn't quite accord with our information. In fact, he told Jack Benn, the Licensee of the White Lion he was coming to see you, two nights ago.

ANDREW. Publicans are notorious opponents of exactitude, Inspector. Vinous gossip is their stock in trade. In particular, I've always found that Jack Benn's observations need constant correction.

DOPPLER. Really, sir. I was wondering if you could correct something else for me.

ANDREW. What's that?

DOPPLER. The impression gained by a man who happened to be passing your house two nights ago, that a fierce struggle was taking place in here.

ANDREW. Does it look like it?

DOPPLER. And that shots were fired?

ANDREW. (uncertainly) Shots?

48

DOPPLER.   Three, our man thinks.

ANDREW.   A car backfiring?

DOPPLER.   No, sir. These were shots. From a gun. Our man is positive.

ANDREW.   May I ask why you took two days to call round and ask me about all this?

DOPPLER.   Well, sir, things take longer to check out than you think. We like to be certain of our facts before troubling a gentleman like yourself.

ANDREW.   Facts? What facts?

DOPPLER.   After our informant reported the incident, we did a spot of checking in the village, and as I say Mr. Benn was very helpful.

ANDREW.   There's an upright citizen, then.

DOPPLER.   Quite so, sir.

ANDREW.   If there were more like him . . .

DOPPLER.   He told us that Mr. Tindle popped into the pub Friday evening for a quick one, and said he was just on his way up to you. Well, what with him being a newcomer to these parts and all, we thought we'd better have a word with him, and see if he could throw any light on the subject. But as I previously indicated he seems to have disappeared, sir.

ANDREW.   But what's that got to do with me?

DOPPLER.   He wasn't at his cottage all of Saturday, nor all today. We must have called half a dozen times.

ANDREW.   By Jove, Merridew would have been proud of you. Now Inspector, if that's all you have to say . . .

DOPPLER.   When we stepped inside Mr. Tindle's cottage to make sure he'd come to no harm, we found this note, sir. (reading) "Urgent we talk. Come Friday night eight o'clock. Wyke." May I ask whether this is your hand-writing, sir?

(DOPPLER shows him the note. ANDREW tries to retain it, but DOPPLER takes it back)

ANDREW.   (trapped) Yes. It's mine alright.

DOPPLER.   So Mr. Tindle was here?

ANDREW.   Yes. The Potman spoke sooth.

DOPPLER.   Perhaps you wouldn't mind answering my original question now, sir.

ANDREW.   Which one?

DOPPLER.   Was there a struggle here two nights ago?

ANDREW.   In a manner of speaking, yes. It was a game we were playing.

DOPPLER.   A game? What kind of game?

ANDREW.   It's rather difficult to explain. It's called Burglary.

DOPPLER.   Please don't joke, sir.

ANDREW.   Isn't it about time you told me I don't know the seriousness of my own position?

DOPPLER.   A man comes here, there is a fight. Shots are heard. He disappears. What would you make of that if you were me?

50

ANDREW. An open and shut case. But things are not always what they seem Inspector. In the case of "The Drowned Dummy" my man, Merridew, once proved by a phonetic mis-spelling the forgery of a document allegedly written by a deaf mute.

DOPPLER. I'm waiting for an explanation.

ANDREW. Tindle arrived at eight and left about an hour and a half later. I haven't seen him since.

DOPPLER. And nor has anyone else, sir.

ANDREW. This is absurd. Are you suggesting that I killed Tindle?

DOPPLER. Killed Tindle, sir. I never mentioned kill.

ANDREW. Oh really! You can't pull that old one on me.

(Joke INSPECTOR's voice)

Garotted, sir? Might I ask how you knew that her ladyship was garotted?

(Normal voice)

Surely *you* told me so Inspector.

(Inspector's voice)

No, sir. I never mentioned it.

DOPPLER. I'm sorry you find us so comic, sir. On the whole what we do is necessary.

ANDREW. "You're just doing your job," that's the over-worked phrase, isn't it?

51

DOPPLER. Possibly, sir. Your wife and Mr. Tindle have been associating closely for some time.

ANDREW. Oh, so you know about that, do you. I suppose you can't keep anything quiet in a small village.

DOPPLER. Perfectly true, sir.

ANDREW. You aren't suggesting a crime passionel, I hope, Inspector—not over Marguerite. It would be like knifing somebody for a table-spoonful of Co-operative White blancmange.

DOPPLER. I'm very partial to blancmange, sir. I find it a great standby.

ANDREW. (oratorically) All of you had either means, motive or opportunity, said Inspector Doppler as he thoughtfully digested another spoonful of his favourite pud. But only one of you had all three.

DOPPLER. Exactly so, sir! That person is you.

ANDREW. Forgive me, Inspector, I suppose I'd better tell you what happened.

DOPPLER. Yes.

ANDREW. Want a bribe to believe it?

DOPPLER. I'll have another drink.

ANDREW. As you seem to know, Tindle was having an affair with my wife. Now, I'm one of that rare breed of men who genuinely don't mind losing gracefully to a gent who's playing by the same rules. But to be worsted by a flash crypto Italian lover, who mistakes my boredom for impotence and my provocative energy for narcissism is too much. It's like starting every game love-30 down, and the Umpire against you.

DOPPLER. You mean you couldn't bring yourself to accept the situation, sir. Is that what you're saying?

ANDREW. I think what infuriated me most was the things he said about me—things that Marguerite repeated to me. I mean no man likes to listen to the other man's witticisms when he's trying to choke down his late night Ovaltine.

DOPPLER. What sort of things, sir?

ANDREW. Oh you know, smarmy, deceitful things which any lover can make about any husband. It's just too easy for them with a captive audience groggy on rediscovered youth and penis envy. (pause) It's not really playing the game.

DOPPLER. You seem to regard marriage as a game, sir.

ANDREW. Not marriage, Inspector. Sex. Sex is the game with marriage the penalty. Round the board we jog towards each futile anniversary. Pass go. Collect 200 rows, 200 silences, 200 scars in the deep places. It's just as well that I don't lack for amorous adventure. Finlandia provides.

DOPPLER. Are you trying to tell me that because of your indifference to your wife, you had no motive for killing Mr. Tindle?

ANDREW. I'm simply saying that in common with most men I want to have my cookie and ignore it.

DOPPLER. Well, sir. I must say you're very frank.

ANDREW. Disarmingly so, I hope.

DOPPLER. Please go on.

ANDREW. As I say. I thought I'd teach Mr. Tindle a lesson for his presumption. In a curious way, some of his remarks which Marguerite repeated to me, led me to

53

believe that he was worth taking a little trouble with—even perhaps worth getting to know. Now, the shortest way to a man's heart is humiliation. You soon find out what he's made of.

DOPPLER. So you invited him here and humiliated him?

ANDREW. I did indeed. I took a leaf out of the book of certain 18th century secret societies. They knew to a nicety how to determine whether someone was worthy to be included amongst their number and also how to humiliate him in the process. I refer of course to the initiation ceremony.

DOPPLER. Would it be something like bullying a new boy at school?

ANDREW. Not unlike, but the victim had the choice of refusal. When Count Cagliastro, the noted magician, sought admission to one such society, he was asked whether he was prepared to die for it, if need be. He said he was. He was then sentenced to death, blindfolded and a pistol containing powder but no shot placed against his temple and discharged.

DOPPLER. And you did this to Mr. Tindle?

ANDREW. More or less. I invited Milo here and suggested to him that as my wife had expensive tastes and he was virtually a pauper, the only course open for him was to steal some valuable jewels which I had in the safe.

DOPPLER. And he agreed to this?

ANDREW. With alacrity. I persuaded him to get out of his clothes and to dress as Grock, in which ludicrous disguise he broke into the house and blew open the safe. He then pocketed the jewels, struggled, convincingly, round this room and was about to make off, when I turned nasty and revealed the purpose of the evening. This, of course,

54

was that I had manoeuvered him into a position where by pretending to mistake him for a burglar, I could, as the outraged householder, legitimately shoot him as he raced away up the stairs. By the time the police arrived I would be standing in my night attire innocent, bewildered and aggrieved. And as you well know, Inspector, there's no liar in Britain, however unconvincing, more likely to be believed than an owner occupier standing with his hair ruffled in front of his own fireplace, wearing striped Viyella pyjamas under a camel Jaeger dressing gown.

DOPPLER.   What was Mr. Tindle's reaction to all this?

ANDREW.   It was electrifying! He swallowed my story hook, line and sinker. He fell on his knees, pleaded for his life, but I was implacable. I put the gun against his head and shot him with a *blank* cartridge. He fainted dead away. It was most gratifying.

DOPPLER.   Gratifying or not, sir. Mr. Tindle must have been put in fear for his life. Such action invites a grave charge of assault.

ANDREW.   Well, I suppose that's marginally better than the murder charge you were comtemplating a few minutes ago.

DOPPLER.   I still am contemplating it, sir.

ANDREW.   Oh come now, Inspector. I've told you what happened. After a few minutes, Mr. Tindle recovered his senses, realised shrewdly that he wasn't dead after all and went off home.

DOPPLER.   (shaking his head in disbelief) Just like that?

ANDREW.   Well, he needed a glass or two of cognac to get the parts working. I mean, wouldn't you?

55

DOPPLER.   I doubt whether I would have survived completely undamaged, sir. The whole thing sounds like the most irresponsible trick.

ANDREW.   Irresponsible? It was quite the contrary. I was upholding the sanctity of marriage. That's more than most people are prepared to do these days. By this action I was clearly stating "Marriage isn't dead. It's alive and well and living in Wiltshire."

DOPPLER.   Tell me, did Mr. Tindle say anything when he left?

ANDREW.   No. He seemed speechless. (laughs) He just lurched off.

DOPPLER.   I'm sorry you appear to find all this so funny, Mr. Wyke. We may not take quite the same attitude.

ANDREW.   Look, why don't you see this from my point of view. In a sense, Milo was a burglar. He was stealing my wife.

DOPPLER.   So you tortured him?

ANDREW.   (exploding) Don't you see. It was a *game!*

DOPPLER.   A game?

ANDREW.   A bloody game, yes!

DOPPLER.   It sounds rather sad, sir—like a child not growing up.

ANDREW.   What's so sad about a child playing, eh!

DOPPLER.   Nothing, sir—if you're a child.

ANDREW.   Let me tell you, Inspector. I have played games of such complexity that Jung and Einstein would have been honoured to have been asked to participate in them. Games of construction and games of destruction. Games of hazard, and games of callidity. Games of deductive logic, inductive logic, semantics, colour association, mathematics, hypnosis and prestidigitation. I have achieved leaps of the mind and leaps of the psyche unknown in ordinary human relationships. And I've had a great deal of not wholly innocent fun.

DOPPLER. And now, sir, you have achieved murder.

ANDREW. No!

DOPPLER. I believe so, sir.

ANDREW. No!!

DOPPLER. Would you mind if I looked around?

ANDREW. Go ahead. Crawl around the floor on hands and knees. Get your envelope out and imprison hairs. Gather ye blunt instruments while ye may.

(DOPPLER rises and starts to examine the room)

(slowly) I ask myself, if I wanted to conceal

(DOPPLER shakes the sailor on his passage round the room)

Milo, where would I put him? In the cellar? Too traditional! In the water tank? . . . Too poisonous! In the linen chest? . . . Too aromatic! In the furnace? . . . Too residual! In the herbaceous border? . . . Too ossiferous! In the . . .

DOPPLER. Excuse me, sir, but these holes in the wall here and here. They look like bullet holes.

ANDREW. (slowly) Quite right, Inspector. So they are.

57

DOPPLER. I understand you to say, sir, that you used a blank.

ANDREW. Two live bullets to set up the trick. One blank to complete it. I had to persuade Tindle I was in earnest. After all, there's really no point in playing a game unless you play it to the hilt.

DOPPLER. I see, sir. One blank. I'd like you to show me where Mr. Tindle was when you killed him.

ANDREW. Pretended to kill him you mean.

DOPPLER. Quite so, sir. Show me, please, exactly where he was when the bullet hit him.

ANDREW. You do realise of course, there wasn't a real bullet.

DOPPLER. (sceptically) Very well, sir. Show me where he was when the blank cartridge was fired.

(ANDREW mounts the stairs followed by the Inspector)

ANDREW. He was standing, kneeling, crouching about here. He fainted and fell down the stairs. Bang!

(DOPPLER passes ANDREW)

DOPPLER. I see. About here you say, sir?

ANDREW. Towards me. Come on. Come on. Stop.

DOPPLER. Were you close to Mr. Tindle when you fired the gun?

ANDREW. Very. I was standing over him in fact, with the gun pressed against his head. The actual feel of the gun coupled with the noise of the explosion was what did the trick. (DOPPLER scrutinizes the staircase) Inspector, I'd like to facilitate your work in every way. Could I interest you in a magnifying glass? No? (DOPPLER bends down to examine the staircase, then the banisters, suddenly he rubs a finger on them, and straightens up, wiping them on his handkerchief)

DOPPLER. Joke blood, sir?

ANDREW. (nervous) I'm not quite sure I follow, Inspector.

DOPPLER. This here on the banisters. It's dried blood.

ANDREW. Blood? Where?

DOPPLER. Here in the angle of the banister—(DOPPLER scrapes some dried blood into an envelope)

(Warily ANDREW crosses to the stairs. He examines the banisters and slowly straightens up. His expression is confused and fearful)

Don't touch it, sir! Oh, look sir, here's some more. Someone's been rubbing at the carpet. Do you see, sir? There, deep in the pile that's blood, sir. Oh! It's still damp. Could you explain how it got there, sir?

ANDREW. I have no idea, Milo . . . er . . . he was a little burnt . . . You must believe me!

DOPPLER. Why should I, sir?

ANDREW. But it's impossible, it was only a game.

DOPPLER. A game, sir? With real bullets and real blood?

ANDREW. (gabbling) There's the hole cut in the pane of glass with the diamond cutter . . . and there are the marks of the ladder on the sill outside . . . and if you look down you'll see the imprint of the other end of the ladder and of size twenty-eight shoes or whatever they were, still there in the flowerbed and this is the bureau that he broke open . . . (DOPPLER descends the stairs)

DOPPLER.   (hard) Thank you, sir, but I don't require a conducted tour. Over the years my eyes have been adequately trained to see things for themselves.

ANDREW.   I'm sure they have, Inspector. I only meant to point out facts which would help substantiate my story. And that's the safe we blew open . . .

DOPPLER.   Where are the jewels now, sir?

ANDREW.   I put them in the bank yesterday.

DOPPLER.   On a Saturday?

ANDREW.   Yes, Inspector, on a Saturday. I went to Salisbury and I put them in the night safe. I felt they'd be better off there. I mean, anyone could break in and steal them.

DOPPLER.   How provident, sir.

ANDREW.   And look down the corridor, you'll see the dressing up basket . . .

(DOPPLER turns away and looks out of the window, over the garden)

DOPPLER.   You didn't point out that mound of earth in the garden, did you, sir?

(ANDREW joins DOPPLER at the window)

ANDREW.   Mound of earth? What mound of earth?

DOPPLER.   Over there—by the far wall. In the shadow of that yew tree. Would you say it had been freshly dug, sir?

ANDREW.   (shouting) How the hell should I know. It's probably something the gardener's doing. A new flowerbed I think he said.

DOPPLER.   A flowerbed under a yew tree, sir?

ANDREW.   (shouting) I've already told you I don't know. Why don't you ask him yourself? He's probably out there somewhere maundering around on his mole-skinned knees aching for an opportunity to slander his employer.

DOPPLER.   Funny, sir. I've always found gardeners make excellent witnesses. Slow, methodical, positive.

ANDREW.   Inspector, I've had just about enough of this farce. Go and dig the damned thing up, if you want to.

DOPPLER.   Oh, we shall, sir. Don't worry.

ANDREW.   (persuasive) Look, do you really think that I'd bury Tindle in the garden, and leave all that newly turned earth for everyone to find?

DOPPLER.   If you weren't expecting us, sir, yes. In a couple of weeks, with some bulbs or a little grass seed, it would be difficult to tell it had ever been disturbed. We in the police know just how fond murderers are of their back gardens, sir.

ANDREW.   (attempts a laugh) You're nearer a killer's heart in a garden than anywhere else on earth, eh?

DOPPLER.   Except a bedroom, sir. I think you'll find that's still favourite.

(DOPPLER starts rummaging in the wardrobe)

Tch! Tch! Tch! What a way to keep your clothes! All screwed up at the back of your wardrobe. Why should you do that, I wonder.

(He holds up Milo's shirt)

That's an interesting monogram. I.W. No, I've got it the wrong way up—M.T.

ANDREW.   Let me see that.

DOPPLER.   (reading) Made by Owen & Smith of Percy Street. 16.8.69 for Mr. Milo Tindle. Tell me something, sir.

(ANDREW seizes the shirt and stares at it in horror, unable to speak. DOPPLER holds up the jacket and carefully reads the name in the inside pocket)

When Mr. Tindle lurched off as you put it, did he lurch naked?

ANDREW.   (in great distress) Believe me, Inspector. I have no idea how those clothes got there.

DOPPLER.   Didn't you tell me that Mr. Tindle stripped off here the other night to disguise himself as a clown?

ANDREW.   Yes, that's right.

DOPPLER.   Another part of the humiliation process, I suppose?

ANDREW.   But he changed back before he left. I mean, you can't really see him walking through the village dressed as a clown, can you?

DOPPLER.   No, sir, I can't. Which makes the appearance of his clothes here all the more significant.

ANDREW.   It's all so difficult . . .

DOPPLER.   On the contrary, sir, I think it's all very simple. I think you started this as a game, exactly as you say you did, in order to play a diabolical trick on Mr. Tindle but that it went wrong. Your third shot was not a blank as

you had supposed, but was in fact a live bullet which killed Mr. Tindle stone dead, spattering his blood on the banisters in the process. When you realised what you'd done, you panicked and simply buried him in the garden. It was silly of you not to wash the blood properly off the banisters and burn his clothes though.

ANDREW. I swear Tindle left here alive.

DOPPLER. I don't believe it.

ANDREW. I didn't murder him.

DOPPLER. I accept that. As I said, I think it happened by accident. We'll be quite content with a charge of manslaughter.

ANDREW. (shouting) I did not kill him! He left here alive.

DOPPLER. If you will pardon a flippancy, sir, you had better tell that to the judge.

ANDREW. Look. There's one way of settling this. If you think Tindle is in the garden, go and dig him up.

DOPPLER. We don't need to find him, sir. Recent decisions have relieved the prosecution of producing the corpus delicti. If Mr. Tindle is not under the newly turned earth in your garden, it will merely go to indicate that in your panic you first thought of putting him there, then changed your mind and buried him somewhere else.

ANDREW. Where?

DOPPLER. Does it matter? Spook Spinney! Flasher's Heath! It's all the same to us. He'll turn up sooner or later—discovered by some adulterous salesman, or rutting boy scout. And if he doesn't it scarcely matters, there's so much circumstantial evidence against you. Come along, it's time to go.

ANDREW.   (a cry) No!

DOPPLER.   I'm afraid I must insist, sir! There's a police car
        outside.

ANDREW.   (louder) You may have a fleet of police cars out
        there. I'm not going.

DOPPLER.   Now let's have no trouble, sir. Please don't make it
        difficult.

ANDREW.   (wildly) I must see a lawyer. It's my right.

        (ANDREW backs away. DOPPLER makes to seize him,
        there is a scuffle)

DOPPLER.   You can make a call from the station, sir. We
        wouldn't want to do anything unconstitutional. Come
        on, sir. Don't despair. At the most you'll only get seven
        years!

ANDREW.   (horrified) Seven years!

DOPPLER.   Seven years to regret playing silly games that go
        wrong.

ANDREW.   (bitterly) It didn't go wrong. It went absolutely
        right. You've trapped me somehow.

DOPPLER.   Yes, sir. You see, we real life detectives aren't as
        stupid as we are sometimes portrayed by writers like
        yourself. We may not have our pipes, or orchid houses,
        our shovel hats or deer-stalkers, but we tend to be
        reasonably effective for all that.

ANDREW.   Who the hell are you?

DOPPLER.   Detective Inspector Doppler, sir, spelt as in C.
        Doppler 1803–1853 whose principle it was that when the
        source of any wave movement is approached, the

frequency appears greater than it would to an observer moving away. It is also not unconnected with Doppler meaning double in German—hence Doppleganger or double image. And of course, for those whose minds run to these things, it is virtually an anagram of the word Plodder. Inspector Plodder becomes Inspector Doppler, if you see what I mean, sir!

ANDREW. (a shriek) Milo!

MILO. (normal voice) The same.

(MILO peels off his disguise which apart from elaborate face and hair make-up—wig, false nose, glasses, cheek padding and moustache, also includes a great deal of body padding, and elevator shoes, which have had the effect of making him taller than ANDREW, where in reality he is a fraction shorter)

ANDREW. You shit!

MILO. Just so.

ANDREW. You platinum plated, copper bottomed, died in the wool, all time knock down dragout, champion bastard Milo!

MILO. Thanks.

ANDREW. You weasel! You cozening coypu!

MILO. Obliged.

ANDREW. You mendacious bollock of Satan. Milo! You triple dealing turd!

MILO. In your debt.

ANDREW. Mind you, I'm not saying it wasn't well done. It was—brilliant.

65

MILO. Thank you.

ANDREW. Have a drink, my dear fellow?

MILO. Let me wash first. I'm covered in make-up and spirit gum.

(ANDREW shakily pours himself a whisky)

ANDREW. Just down the corrdior. Cheers!

MILO. Good health. (MILO exits to the bathroom upstage left as Andrew gulps it down)

ANDREW. Yes, I must say, Milo, I congratulate you. It was first class. You really had me going there for a moment.

MILO. (offstage, quizzically) For a moment?

ANDREW. For a long moment I concede. Of course, I had my suspicions towards the end. Flasher's Heath indeed! That was going a bit far.

MILO. (offstage) I was giving you one of your English sporting chances.

ANDREW. What did you think of my performance? The anguish of an innocent man trapped by circumstantial evidence.

MILO. (offstage) Undignified—if it was a performance.

(MILO returns on stage, picks up his clothes)

ANDREW. Of course it was, and it had to be undignified to be convincing. As I say, I had my suspicions.

MILO. Indeed? How cleverly you kept them to yourself.
(MILO goes upstairs to the wardrobe where he dresses in his own clothes)

ANDREW. And how well you executed it. I loved your
Inspector Doppler. His relentless courtesy, his chilly
rusticity, his yeoman beadiness.

MILO. (DOPPLER voice) I'm glad you view the trifling
masquerade in that light, sir.

ANDREW. He was quite a masterpiece: Inspector Ringrose
crossed with a hint of declasse Roger Sheringham I'd have
said.

MILO. Really?

ANDREW. Oh yes. Surely you remember the Poisoned
Chocolates Case 1929. It was a really astounding tour de
force with no less than six separate solutions.

MILO. I've never heard of it.

ANDREW. You should read it. It's a veritable textbook of the
literature. Not that you need any tips on plotting. I
suppose you slipped in here when I was over in Salisbury?

MILO. Yes, I waited to see you leave.

ANDREW. And dumped the clothes in the wardrobe, and
sprinkled a little sacrificial blood on the banisters.

MILO. Exactly. But it wasn't my blood you will be relieved to
hear. It was obtained from a pig's liver.

ANDREW. Ugh! Perhaps you will do me the favour of wiping
it off in a minute. I don't wish to fertilise the woodworm.

MILO. Question. Where would you find homosexual
woodworms?

ANDREW. What?

MILO. In a tallboy.

67

(ANDREW grimaces. MILO comes downstairs)

(sharply) I'd like that drink now.

ANDREW.   Yes, of course. (ANDREW goes to drinks table and pours a brandy for MILO) You deserve it.

MILO.   (sits on chair under staircase) You know I haven't congratulated you on your game yet. You brought it off with great elan.

ANDREW.   Did you think so? Oh good! Good! I must say I was rather delighted with it myself. Tell me . . . did you really think that your last moment on earth had come?

MILO.   Yes.

ANDREW.   You're not angry, are you?

MILO.   Anger is a meaningless word in this context.

ANDREW.   I've already tried to explain it to you. I wanted to get to know you—to see if you were, as I suspected, my sort of person.

MILO.   A games-playing sort of person?

ANDREW.   Exactly.

MILO.   And am I?

ANDREW.   Most certainly. There's no doubt about it.

MILO.   And what exactly is a games-playing person?

ANDREW.   He's the complete man—a man of reason and imagination; of potent passions and bright fancies. He's joyous and unrepenting. His weapons are the openness of a child and the cunning of a pike and with them he faces out the black terrors of life. For me personally he is a

68

man who dares to live his life without the crutch of domestic tension. You see, at bottom, I'm rather a solitary man. An arrangement of clouds, the secret mystery of landscape, a game of intrigue and revelation, mean more to me than people—even the ones I'm supposed to be in love with. I've never met a woman to whom the claims of intellect were as absolute as they are to me. For a long time I was reticent about all this, knowing that most people would mistake my adroit heart for one of polished stone. But it doesn't worry me any longer. I'm out in the open. I've turned my whole life into one great work of happy invention.

MILO. And you think I'm like this?

ANDREW. Yes, I do.

MILO. You're wrong.

ANDREW. I'm not. Look at the way you chose to get back at me—by playing Inspector Doppler.

MILO. That was just the need for revenge. Every Italian knows about that.

ANDREW. Rubbish. You could have revenged yourself in one of many crude Mafiosi ways—cutting off the gardener's hands, for example, or staking the cleaning woman out on the gravel, or even I suppose, as a last resort, scratched loutish words on the bonnet of my Lagonda. But no, you had to resort to a game.

MILO. I like to pay back in kind.

ANDREW. And is honour satisfied? Is it one set all?

MILO. (hard) By no means. Your game was superior to mine. I merely teased you for a few minutes with the thought of prison. (low) You virtually terrified me to death.

69

ANDREW. My dear fellow . . .

MILO. (slowly, thinking it out) And that changes you profoundly. Once you've given yourself to death, actually faced the fact that the coat sleeve button, the banister, the nail on your fourth finger, are the last things you're going to see ever—and then *heard* the sound of your own death—things cannot be the same again. I feel I've been tempered by madness. I stand outside and see myself for the first time without responsibility.

ANDREW. (nervous) That's shock, my dear chap. It'll pass. Here, have another drink. (ANDREW reaches for the glass. MILO jerks away. He is in great distress) How cold you are. Milo, my dear fellow, I didn't realise how absolutely cold . . .

MILO. So that my only duty is to even our score. That's imperative. As you would put it "I'm three games up in the second set, having lost the first six love." That's right, isn't it? That's about how you see it? I should hate to cheat.

ANDREW. You're being too modest, Milo. In my scoring it's one set all.

MILO. Oh no, I can't accept that. You see to the ends of playing the game and drawing honourably level, I *have* killed someone.

ANDREW. Killed someone?

MILO. Murdered someone. Committed murder.

ANDREW. You're not serious.

MILO. Yes.

ANDREW. What is this. Some new murder game?

70

MILO. Yes. But it has a difference. Both the game and the murder are real. There's absolutely no point in another pretence murder game, is there?

ANDREW. (soothing) No, none. But I don't like to take advantage of you in this emotional state.

MILO. (shouting) It can't wait.

ANDREW. (soothing) Alright. Alright. Let's play your game. Who did you kill?

MILO. Your girlfriend, Tēa . . .

ANDREW. You killed Tēa?

MILO. (a little giggle) She whose cobalt eyes were the secret forest pools of Finlandia. I closed them.

ANDREW. You . . .

MILO. I strangled her—right here on this rug I strangled her and . . . I had her first.

ANDREW. You raped and str . . .

MILO. No. Not rape. She wanted it.

ANDREW. You're lying. You can't take me in with a crude game like this. (with braggadocio) Honestly, Milo. You're in the big league now. I gave you credit for better sport than this.

MILO. You'll have all the sport you can stomach in a moment, Andrew. That I promise you.

ANDREW. Really, Milo, I think it would be better if . . .

MILO. When I was here yesterday, planting the blood and clothes for my Inspector Doppler scene, Tēa called. I strangled her. She was under that freshly dug mound of earth in the garden that so took Doppler's fancy.

ANDREW. Was? You mean she's not there now?

MILO. No. I moved her.

ANDREW. (derisory) You moved her? Where to? Flasher's Heath I suppose.

MILO. Something like that. It was too easy leaving her here . . . Too easy for the game you are going to play against the clock before the police arrive.

ANDREW. The police?

MILO. Yes. You see, about an hour ago I 'phoned them up and asked them to meet me here at ten o'clock tonight. They should be here in about ten minutes.

ANDREW. (sarcastic) Yes, yes. I'm sure they will be. Led, no doubt, by intrepid downy Inspector Doppler.

MILO. Oh no. It'll be a real policeman, have no fear of that. Detective Sergeant Tarrant his name is. I told him a lot about you, Andrew, I said that I knew you to be a man obsessed with games-playing and murder considered as a fine art. Your life's great ambition, I said, of which you'd often spoken, was to commit an actual real life murder, hide the body somewhere where it couldn't be traced to you and then leave clues linking you with the crime, strewn about your house in the certain knowledge that the pedestrian and simple-minded police wouldn't recognise them for what they were.

ANDREW. Obsessed with games-playing and murder considered as a fine art! That's rather ingenious of you, Milo. But it won't work. Please sir, Andrew Wyke can't rest until he's committed a real murder which is going to make fools out of all you coppers. Honestly! Tell that to the average desk Sergeant and you'll find yourself strapped straight into the giggle jacket.

MILO.   Not so in fact, I told them that if they didn't believe me, one look at your bookcase and the furnishings of your house would confirm what I said about your obsessions.

ANDREW.   (slow) Go on.

MILO.   I also told them that two days ago your girlfriend had come to my house in great distress saying you suspected she was having affairs with other men and had threatened to kill her.

ANDREW.   The police believed all that?

MILO.   After some demur, yes.

ANDREW.   The fuzz are watching too much T.V.

MILO.   You mustn't resent imagination in public office, Andrew. Of course, I went on I had no proof that any harm had actually been done to her, but I thought I had better report the matter, particularly as I had just received an excited phone call from you, Andrew, saying you were all set to achieve your life's great ambition.

ANDREW.   My dear boy, I quite appreciate you have been captivated by the spirit of games-playing and the need as you see it, to get even, but frankly you are trying too hard to be a big boy, too soon.

(ANDREW goes to the telephone and dials)

Hello, Joyce, this is Andrew. May I speak to Tēa . . . she what? . . . when was this? Where . . . ? Oh my God!

(ANDREW replaces the receiver and takes a drink straight from the bottle. MILO is very excited)

73

MILO. I told you. I killed her yesterday. Now sweat for your life. You have a little over ten minutes before the law arrives. It's your giant brain against their plodding ones. Concealed in this room are two incriminating clues. And as a final expression of your contempt for the police you hid the murder weapon itself. Do you follow me so far?

ANDREW. (admiringly) You bastard!

MILO. No judgements please. Three objects. Those you don't find, be sure the police will. I should add that they're all in plain view though I have somewhat camouflaged them to make the whole thing more fun. The first object is a crystal bracelet.

ANDREW. Not . . .

MILO. Yes, I tore it off her wrist . . . off you go. It's inscribed "From Andrew to Tēa, a propitiary offering to a Karelian Goddess."

ANDREW. Alright! Alright! I know how it's inscribed.

(ANDREW takes off his jacket and starts his search)

MILO. Would you like some help?

ANDREW. Yes, damn you!

MILO. Tch! Tch! . . . For any man with half an eye
What stands before him may espy;
But optics sharp it needs I ween,
To see what is not to be seen.

ANDREW. (furious) You said everything was in plain view.

MILO. Well, it's paradoxical old me, isn't it?

74

ANDREW. I'll get my own back for this . . . don't worry.
That I promise you. I'll roast you for this . . . I'll make
you so sorry you ever . . .

MILO. Eight minutes.

ANDREW. (slowly to himself) I must think . . . I must think
. . . It's in plain view, yet not to see seen. H'm . . .
there's a visual trick involved.

(ANDREW searches the stage)

MILO A propitiary offering, eh! What was it you had to
propitiate for I ask myself?

ANDREW. None of your bloody business.

MILO. Just being yourself I suppose. Just for being cold,
torturing, Andrew Wyke. Poor Tēa, I wonder if all her
jewellery was inscribed with apologies for your bully boy
behaviour.

ANDREW. That's a cheap jibe.

MILO. Mind you, at least you gave her some. Marguerite just
had the use of them.

ANDREW. I see what you're doing. You're trying to distract
me . . . But you won't succeed . . . I'll solve your puzzle
. . . Let me think . . . Optics sharp it needs to see what
is not to be seen . . . with the naked eye? It's
microscopic! You only see a fraction of it. That's it!

(ANDREW picks up the microscope and uses it)

MILO. You won't need the Sherlock Holmes kit, Andrew. The
bracelet is full sized and in full view. Though the
detective angle is not a bad one. I wonder how your man,
Merry*dick*, would have gone about the search.

75

ANDREW. (furious) Merrydew! St. Lord John Merrydew!

MILO. Perhaps he'd have clambered up on to that desk to look at the plinth, hauling his great tun of port belly after him.

(ANDREW climbs up on his desk to inspect the plinth)

Or perhaps he'd have gone straight to the chimney and shoved his fat Father Christmas face right up it.

(ANDREW runs to the chimney and climbs inside it)

My God! cried the noble Lord, puking on his pipe and indulging his famed taste for bad puns. This is hardly a *sootable* place for a gentleman!

(ANDREW emerges from the chimney)

ANDREW. I won't listen to you. I must think . . . What are the properties of crystal? It's hard . . . It's brilliant . . . It's transparent.

MILO. You're getting warm, Andrew.

ANDREW. You look through it and you don't see it. Now the only place to conceal a transparent thing, so as to make it invisible yet keep it in plain view, is in another transparent thing like . . .

(ANDREW inspects various glass objects including Milo's drink which he is holding conspicuously. Finally he crosses to the ornamental tank, downstage right and lifts out the bracelet)

Suddenly it's all as clear as crystal. I don't need to destroy this, do I? She could have this here any time.

MILO.   True, it was only planted so that the police could read
the inscription. At least they'd know that your
relationship with Tēa hadn't always been a happy one.

ANDREW.   Very subtle. What next?

MILO.   The next object is much more damning. The clue is a
riddle, which goes as follows:

Two brothers we are,
Great burdens we bear,
On which we are bitterly pressed.
The truth is to say,
We are full all the day,
And empty when we go to rest.

ANDREW.   Oh, I know that . . . don't tell me . . . full all the
day, empty when we go to rest . . . it's a . . . it's a pair
of shoes!

MILO.   Very good. In this case, one right, high-heeled shoe. Size
6. The other, I need hardly add, is on Tēa's body.

ANDREW.   Oh, my God. Poor Tēa.

(ANDREW searches the room)

MILO.   Poor Tēa, eh? Well, that's a bit better. It's the first sign
of sorrow you've shown since you heard of her death.

ANDREW.   It's not true! You think I don't care about Tēa,
don't you? But I must save myself.

MILO.   You're loving it. You're in a high state of brilliance and
excitement. The thought that you are playing a game for
your life is practically giving you an orgasm. It's pitiable.

ANDREW.   Hold your filthy tongue. What you see before you
is someone using a mighty control to keep terror in check,

77

while he tries to solve a particularly sadistic and morbid puzzle. It's a triumph of the mind over atavism!

(ANDREW searches under the stairs and in the bookshelves, and pipe racks then the sailor's foot and finally finds the shoe in a brightly decorated cornucopia attached to the stage left column)

Ah! What have we here?

MILO.   Very good! Sorry it's so messy. It's only earth from Tēa's first grave in your garden.

(ANDREW burns the shoe in the stove)

ANDREW.   Now there's one thing left, isn't there. The murder weapon, that's what you said. Now you strangled her here. What with? Let's see . . . a rope . . . a belt . . . a scarf . . .

MILO.   It bit into her neck very deeply, Andrew. I had to prise it loose.

ANDREW.   You sadistic bloody wop!

MILO.   I hope I didn't hear that correctly . . . It would be foolish to antagonise me at this stage. Because as you're certain to need a lot more help, I would hate to have to give you an oblique, Florentine sort of clue, sewn with treachery and double dealing.

ANDREW.   (controlling himself) Alright! Alright!

MILO.   As Don Quixote in common with a great number of chaps remarked, "No es Oro todo que reluce."

ANDREW.   But the other chaps of course, didn't say it in Spanish, did they?

MILO.   Well at least you know it was Spanish, even if you can't speak it. I suppose that's what is meant by a general education in England.

ANDREW.   God, you're pretty damned insufferable, Milo.

MILO.   I've learnt it. Let's try you on a little Latin. Every gentleman knows Latin. I'm sure you're acquainted with the Winchester College Hall Book of 1401?

ANDREW.   (sarcastic) Naturally. As a matter of fact I've got the paperback by my bedside.

MILO.   (bland) Then you will remember an entry by Alanus De Insulis—"Non teneas nurum totum quod splendet ut aurum."

ANDREW.   (sarcastic) I'm afraid I can't have got that far yet.

MILO.   Pity . . . I suppose I could put it another way. "Que tout n'est pas or qu'on voit luire." The French, of course, is thirteenth century.

ANDREW.   Say it again, slowly.

MILO.   All-that-glitters . . .

ANDREW.   All that glitters isn't gold . . . Why didn't you say that in the first place . . .

(MILO whistles a scale)

Golden notes? Golden whistle? . . . Golden cord? . . . Golden cord! You strangled her with a golden cord and put it round the bell pull.

(ANDREW runs to the bell pull, examines it, but finds nothing)

No you didn't.

(MILO whistles "Anything Goes")

Anything goes. In olden d . . . In olden days a . . .
glimpse of stocking. It's in the spin dryer.

(ANDREW goes off down corridor to kitchen)

MILO.   Cold, cold. It's in this room remember.

ANDREW.   Where do you put stockings? On legs, golden
legs . . .

(ANDREW examines the golden legs of the fender, then
a chair)

MILO.   (sings) "In olden days a glimpse of stocking was looked
on as something shocking . . ." I thought I heard
something.

(MILO exits to hallway. MILO comes back on stage)

Yes, Andrew, it's the police. They're coming up the drive.

ANDREW.   (desperate) Keep them out! Give me one more
minute!

MILO.   A glimpse of stocking, remember.

(MILO exits to hallway)

(offstage) Good evening. Detective Sergeant Tarrant.

DET. SGT. TARRANT.   Yes, sir. This is Constable Higgs.

MILO.   Good evening, Constable.

CON. HIGGS.   Good evening, sir.

(The grandfather clock strikes 10:00)

ANDREW. Olden days . . . A glimpse . . . Now you see it now you don't! Of course, the clock.

(He rushes to clock and finds stocking)

MILO. Nice of you to be so prompt. I apologise for keeping you waiting out there for a moment. The front door's a bit stiff.

TARRANT. That's alright, sir. We're used to waiting.

MILO. Won't you hang your coats up? It's a bit warm inside.

TARRANT. Thank you, sir. I expect we'll be here a little time.

(ANDREW puts stocking into fire)

MILO. Here, Constable. Let me take your helmet.

HIGGS. Thank you, sir. If it's all the same to you, I think I'll keep it with me, but I'll take my coat off. (Door slams offstage. ANDREW runs to his desk and sits unconcernedly reading)

MILO. Come in, gentlemen. May I introduce Mr. Andrew Wyke. Andrew, may I introduce Detective Sergeant Tarrant and Constable Higgs.

ANDREW. Come in, gentlemen, come in.

(A pause. No one enters)

MILO. Or perhaps I should say Inspector Plodder and Constable Freshface. Thank you, Sergeant. We won't be needing you after all.

TARRANT'S VOICE. That's alright, sir. Better to be safe than sorry, that's what I say. Good night, sir.

MILO.   (own voice) Good night, Sergeant. Good night, Constable. Good night, sir.

(ANDREW sinks on the settee, shattered)

Aren't you going to ask about Tēa? She did call here yesterday looking for you when I was here setting the Doppler scene. I told her about the trick you had played on me with the gun. She wasn't a bit surprised. She knows only too well the kind of games you play—the kind of humiliation you enjoy inflicting on people. I said I wanted to play a game to get even with you and I asked her to help me. I asked her to lend me a stocking, a shoe and a bracelet. She collaborated with enthusiasm. So did her flat-mate, Joyce. Would you like to telephone her, she'll talk to you now? Of course you don't really have much to say to her, do you? She's not really your mistress. She told me you and she hadn't slept together for over a year. She told me you were practically impotent—not at all, in fact, the selector's choice for the next Olympics.

(ANDREW hides his head as MILO starts up the stairs)

ANDREW.   Where are you going?

MILO.   To collect Marguerite's fur coat.

ANDREW.   She's not coming back?

MILO.   No. Among other things she said she was fed up with living in Hamleys.

ANDREW.   Hamleys?

MILO.   It's a toy shop in Regent Street.

ANDREW.   Milo.

MILO.   Yes?

82

ANDREW. Don't go. Don't waste it all on Marguerite. She doesn't appreciate you like I do. You and I are evenly matched. We know what it is to play a game and that's so rare. Two people coming together who have the courage to spend the little time of light between the eternal darkness—joking.

MILO. Do you mean live here?

ANDREW. Yes.

MILO. (scornfully) Is it legal in private between two consenting games-players?

ANDREW. Please . . . I just want someone to play with.

MILO. No.

ANDREW. Please.

MILO. No. Most people want someone to live with. But you have no life to give anyone—only tricks and the shadows of long ago. Take a look at yourself, Andrew, and ask yourself a few simple questions about your attachment to the English detective story. Perhaps you might come to realise that the only place you can inhabit is a dead world—a country house world where peers and colonels die in their studies; where butlers steal the port, and pert parlourmaids cringe, weeping malapropisms behind green baize doors. It's a world of coldness and class hatred, and two dimensional characters who are not expected to communicate; it's a world where only the amateurs win, and where foreigners are automatically figures of fun. To be *puzzled* is all. Forgive me for taking Marguerite to a life where people try to *understand*. To put it shortly, the detective story is the normal recreation of snobbish, out-dated, life hating, ignoble minds. I'll get that fur coat now. I presume it is Marguerite's, unless, that is, you've taken to transvestism as a substitute for non-performance.

(MILO disappears into the bedroom. ANDREW sits
on below, crushed and humiliated. After a minute, he
rises and starts wearily across the stage. Suddenly he stops
as a thought enters his mind)

ANDREW.   (to himself) The coat! . . . The fur coat . . . of
course . . . I've got him!

(He brightens visibly—a man who realises suddenly
that he can rescue a victory out of the jaws of
defeat—and crosses firmly to his desk and takes out his
gun)

You see, Inspector, I was working in the morning room
when I heard a noise. I seized my gun and came in here.
I saw the figure of a man, apparently carrying my wife's
fur coat. I shouted for him to put his hands up, but
instead he ran towards the front door, trying to escape.
Though I aimed low, I'm afraid I shot him dead.

(INSPECTOR's voice) Mustn't blame yourself, sir,
could have happened to anybody!

(MILO returns carrying fur coat. He comes down the
stairs, but does not see the gun hidden behind
ANDREW's back)

I'm not going to let you go, you know.

MILO.   No? What are you going to do, Andrew. Shoot me
down? Play that old burglar game again?

ANDREW.   Yes, that's precisely what I could do.

MILO.   It wouldn't work, you know, even if you had the guts to
go through with it.

ANDREW.   Why not?

(MILO fetches a suitcase from the hall and packs the fur
coat)

MILO.   Because of what happened when I left here on Friday
          night. I lurched home in the moonlight, numb and
          dazed, and soiled. I sat up all night in a chair—
          damaged—contaminated by you and this house. I
          remembered something my father said to me; "In this
          country, Milo" he said, "there's justice, but sometimes for
          a foreigner it is difficult." In the morning I went to the
          police station and told them what had happened. One of
          them—Sergeant Tarrant—yes he's real—took me into a
          room and we had quite a long chat. But I don't think he
          really believed me, even though I showed him the powder
          burn on my head. He seemed more interested in my
          relationship with Marguerite, which by the way they all
          appeared to know about. I felt this terrible anger coming
          over me. I thought "they're not going to believe me
          because I'm a stranger from London who's screwing the
          wife of the local nob and has got what he deserved." So I
          thought of my father, and what I might have done in
          Italy, and I took my own revenge. But remember,
          Andrew, the police might still come.

ANDREW.   (slowly) Then why haven't they, then?

MILO.   I don't know, perhaps they won't. But even if they
          don't, you can't play your burglar game now, they'd never
          swallow it. So you see you've lost.

ANDREW.   I don't believe one word you're saying.

MILO.   (deliberately) It's the truth.

ANDREW.   You're lying.

MILO.   Why don't you 'phone Sergeant Tarrant if you don't
          believe me.

ANDREW.   And say what? Please Sergeant has Milo Tindle
          been in saying that I framed him as a burglar and then
          shot him. I'm not that half-witted.

MILO.   Suit yourself.

ANDREW.   I shall shoot you, Milo. You come here and ask my
permission to steal away my wife, you pry into my
manhood, you lecture me on dead worlds and ignoble
minds, and you mock Merridew. Well, they're all real
bullets this time.

MILO.   I'm going home now.

(MILO starts to leave, Andrew fires at the last moment.
MILO staggers downstage right and drops in pain,
fatally. ANDREW kneels and holds his head up)

ANDREW.   You're a bad liar, Milo, and in the final analysis, an
uninventive games-player. Can you hear me? Then listen
to this, NEVER play the same game three times
running!

(There is the sound of a car approaching and pulling to a
halt. A flashy blue police car light shines through the
window. The doorbell rings. Loud knocking on door.
Painfully MILO lifts his head from the floor, he laughs)

MILO.   Game, set and match!

(His laugh becomes a cough. Blood trickles from his
mouth. He grimaces in surprise at the pain and dies. The
knocking on the door is repeated more loudly.
ANDREW staggers to his desk and accidentally presses
the button on it. This sets off the sailor who laughs
ironically. The knocking becomes more insistent.
ANDREW leans weakly against pillar as the curtain
falls)